The Restaurant Survival Bible

"Starting and operating a successful restaurant is complex business and Bill makes it fascinating. His compelling stories of victories and defeats interwoven with solid inside info about the biz is dynamic writing that you won't be able to put down." Tony Levin, author, publisher and musican.

"Bill's book is witty, well written & all too true. Made me wonder why I got into this business in the first place." Jon Rothkopf, owner & head busboy, Landau Grill, Woodstock, NY

"Bill's Survival Bible offers a reliable formula for successfully navigating the shark-filled waters of restaurant entreprenurialism. His own personal slings and arrows provide a hip, honest, and, most importantly, objective view of the perils and pleasures of owning and operating a successful restaurant." Eric Mann, Chef and Co-owner of The Bear Café, Woodstock, NY.

"Billy does it his way and the bottom line is that it works. Let him show you how-and even more important, how not to-open your restaurant." Peter Cantine, Co-owner of The Bear Café, Woodstock, NY

The Restaurant Survival Bible

An Insider's Guide to Successful and Profitable Restaurant Ownership

William J. Durkin

Writers Club Press
San Jose New York Lincoln Shanghai

The Restaurant Survival Bible
An Insider's Guide to Successful and Profitable Restaurant Ownership

All Rights Reserved © 2000 by William J. Durkin

No part of this book may be reproduced or transmitted in any form or by any means, graphic, electronic, or mechanical, including photocopying, recording, taping, or by any information storage retrieval system, without the permission in writing from the publisher.

Writers Club Press
an imprint of iUniverse.com, Inc.

For information address:
iUniverse.com, Inc.
620 North 48th Street, Suite 201
Lincoln, NE 68504-3467
www.iuniverse.com

Any references to historical events; to real people, living or dead; or to real locales are intended only to give a sense of reality and authenticity. Names, characters, places, and incidents either are the product of the author's imagination or are used fictitiously, and their resemblance, if any, to real-life counterparts is entirely coincidental.

ISBN: 0-595-14083-1

Printed in the United States of America

This book is dedicated to all those who plan to sail the difficult and rewarding waters of the restaurant business.

Contents

Acknowledgements ix
An "I'll Betcha" Restaurant Story xi
1. Why Would You Want to Do This? 1
2. The "Mom and Pop" Way of Doing It 7
3. What Are You Bringing to the Party? 15
4. Location. Location. Location. 26
5. What to Do Right Away to Avoid the Big One! 39
6. The Business Plan 46
7. Dealing for the Ideal Deal 52
8. Our Budget 60
9. Our Concept 72
10. Fine Tuning All Systems for Takeoff 90
11. The Rehearsal Week 116
12. I.R.S.—I Rest Soundly 131
13. Restaurant Divorce 139
14. P. S.—To Summarize 146
About the Author 169

Acknowledgements

Special thanks to Doug McGilvray for his help in preparing this manuscript and to Eric Brown for his cover art and title illustrations for each chapter. I especially want to thank my wife, Mariann Durkin, from the bottom of my heart for her love and support during the writing of this book.

An "I'll Betcha" Restaurant Story

On a dreary, freezing, rainy night I was sitting at the bar in my restaurant (a very small bar, I should point out), talking to some people when in came a man I'd known as a customer for some time. He was an older man from India who did business in New York City and on weekends in Woodstock in the Catskill Mountains. On this particular evening he was celebrating his buying of the closed restaurant property that was the doormat to our town, and which still had, for some, the luster and fantasy of days gone by when it was the roaring "Deanies" of the '60s, '70s and early '80s. The new buyer had a drink and a bit loudly offered me first chance at some type of partnership with him in his new venture. I invited him to my office and listened to him rave on about his plans for succeeding in a business in which he had no experience. I listened and listened. Then it occurred to me that he would no longer be a customer of mine but, rather, the competition, and his arrogance was wearing thin. So in a matter of fact way, I told him all the reasons I passed on the deal three years before at a very reduced price compared to what he was paying. He didn't hear a word I said but became defensive and took his money out of his pocket and waved it at me yelling, "I bet you five thousand dollars I win and if I don't, I know how to get out!"

I thought laughing at the whole situation was the best way out and I wished him well as he left the room.

Unbeknownst to me, my wife, Mariann, and some friends were having a post movie glass of wine at "The Bear Café," our town's best fine dining house, when she encountered the guy who had just left my office. When he saw Mariann he told her that I was a negative person and so he was offering the same deal to the owners of "The Bear." My wife listened to his version of our conversation and told him quite simply that I knew a little about the restaurant business and maybe he should appreciate my opinions because of my restaurant experience and his lack of it.

This guy eventually asked every local restaurant owner to become his partner. Although the arrangements he offered were ridiculous, some people joined him in his effort. That relationship lasted two months as did every relationship this guy had with anyone in town, whether they were working for him or with him. He and his friends/partners put a ton of money into the remodeling of the place, yet he owed balances to different contractors that he kept. He was dead in the water months before he would open. Poison your well in this business and you are doomed. Lose your local clientele and you lose.

But that didn't stop this guy. He continued to alienate the working people of this town and they badmouthed him worse than lousy weather. He owed town merchants and they gossiped that his funeral would be well attended within less than a year—meaning that they wanted their money. Sales tax people wanted their money. Employees and contractors wanted their money. As customers went elsewhere, he began doing desperate things to duck the bill collectors. The doors closed, Chapter Eleven papers were filed and many town businesses were burned for various sums. A month later the bank foreclosed on the guy's house.

All this took less than a year. It was the third time this had happened since I've been in Woodstock and yet at this writing another individual has taken the spot and done a costly makeover of the place. Soon he will open the doors of his *first* restaurant. I'll betcha the results are the same. Why? Most people don't do their homework in this business, by which I mean freezing an impulse to open a restaurant while asking themselves the hard questions.

This book is about what we need to do and not do in this business, so that when we want to be owner-operators we have the best shot at succeeding.

What didn't happen at the old "Deanies" location is obvious. No national or regional operators took more than a cursory look at the property. Neither did smaller successful local operators. They all passed on the situation after doing their various homework exercises that told them it would not be a successful venture. A lot of experience and expertise went into their Not Possible analysis. Their number crunching ended their interest.

That's the bottom line dollar part of the restaurant business. The human element brought to the restaurant business is more complex and complicated. But when people do their homework, and bring the right experience and expertise to a well-planned effort, these dynamics can make it succeed.

CHAPTER 1

Why would you want to DO this?

1. Why Would You Want to Do This?

No business pursuit I know of is as loaded with misconceptions, wrong assumptions and personal tragedies as the restaurant business. The food business is the biggest business in the world. The food service industry in the United States is in excess of $400 billion annually—making the restaurant part of the industry the most demanding and dangerous segment. The failure rate is astounding. Some sources say 90%, others say 60 to 75%, yet people continue to pursue this most difficult and sometimes rewarding business.

Why that is I'll never know. Maybe it has something to do with the fact that we use restaurants all the time and assume that if they can do it so can we. Maybe the glamour associated with certain restaurants has lured someone to give it a try. Perhaps restaurant experiences or a culinary education made us into wannabe restaurant owners. No matter what the reasons (or excuses) people use to go in and out of the restaurant business one factor remains constant: the restaurant business is a high risk business where the bottom line profit of ten cents on a dollar is considered success.

The "Mom and Pop" restaurant concept dates back to the married couple that owned and operated the restaurant on Noah's Ark. It doesn't matter how the Mom and Pop team is configured. What matters is that the idea of owner-operators is understood. In today's restaurant marketplace, great things can be done but rarely can these things be done individually. It takes two different personality types to accomplish a shared goal in the Mom and Pop niche. One is the back of the house producer of appreciated meals and the other is the front of the house producer of good service with meaningful "Hellos," "How are you doing?" "Thank you" and "Goodbye." It's not easy to do. Restaurant marriages are something else, yet when they work, they can be very rewarding. That's what this book is about: making it work and how to avoid being in restaurant situations that don't work.

What is really unique in the restaurant business is the warning sign found in every food service business around the world. It's a plaque about the size of a business card located by the kitchen door, inscribed with the following:

> **WARNING!**
> **All who enter here are doomed to a nightmare of endless toil for little, if any, reward. Say goodbye to sleep, family and friends.**
> **Prepare for sale your soul to the Devil to leave here.**

Is the warning too harsh? I don't think so because the warning only has to do with the working aspect of the business. The harsh reality of the money part of starting a restaurant is much worse than the hard work.

Unless you're a trust fund baby with unlimited money you'll more than likely use your savings and then beg, borrow and promise back with interest funds from family, friends and long lost relatives. If by chance your effort goes down in flames, the pain of failure coupled with debts owed is unbearable and extracts a tremendous toll until debts are satisfied. It's that harsh but true, and I've been there. Failure in this business ruins lives and relationships.

After a restaurant disaster, there is money owed, hurt feelings and a lot of hiding and lying. This book does not guarantee that failure will not occur. But if it does, you'll walk away not buried in debt and misery but ready to go again *stronger than ever.*

I'm one of those people born into a family-run restaurant business. After that, I always worked in other restaurants. Through high school, college and graduate school, restaurant work always afforded me a living.

Even during my acting career I was always a waiter, bartender or cook by night. But it wasn't until the early 1980s in New York City that I saw my first Warning Plaque.

Growing up in the restaurant business must have some drawbacks but the experience over the years has become invaluable and has led me to many successes. But that experience isn't what led me to write this book. What got me into this was watching two sets of friends go down in their attempts to open restaurants. I'll spare you the details of their demise because neither was pleasant. I did spend time with them and I thought they were listening and benefiting from my input but they did not. Why was that? I've thought a lot about this and feel that they simply didn't get it and they didn't hear it because they didn't know what they wanted! They knew everything except what they really wanted and because they didn't know what they really wanted, they didn't know what they were doing.

For example, I could say I wanted to go sailing and I could buy a nice sailing boat but that doesn't make me a sea-worthy sailor. And if I started out on an ocean crossing, I'd be lost, nearly dead or dead within a couple of weeks. But you could throw an experienced sea captain into the raging seas in a dingy and within days he'd be saved or make land. So if I really wanted to sail I'd find someone like that sea captain to learn from.

It's the same thing in the restaurant business. By reading this book you'll learn how to sail safely through the shark-infested waters of the Mom and Pop Restaurant World.

The restaurant business is like the contracting business in the sense that it is a catchall for every imaginable personality-type. A person can go to the hardware store buy a tool belt, some power tools, and the next thing you know he's a general contractor screwing up someone's house.

Just because we all use restaurants and are, therefore, very familiar with them, does not mean we, as diners, can run and operate a restaurant. Nor can restaurant employees do it. Nor can graduates of culinary schools. Believe me, they can't!

I've worked in so many situations with all the different "wannabe" restaurant owners and almost without exception they fail. Why? Because knowing a little about the restaurant business is just that, a little. It's the not knowing all the other components of owning and operating a restaurant that ultimately cause the heartache of failure. Can anything be done to avoid these problems?

I believe that the burning focal point of our desire to accomplish our goals is clearly in knowing what we want. This knowledge forges all our energies, creativity and resources into a resolve which moves us towards accomplishing what we want by allowing us to focus on the total picture of the world we are about to create. Knowing what you want and seeing the total picture empowers you to learn how your intended business must work. When you arrive at an understanding of this concept, this book will serve you well. Think about what you want and if owning and operating a restaurant is it and you're willing to work through these lessons with me, you'll learn the following from this book:

1. How to avoid the costly mistakes of being beaten in a tough game.
2. How to acquire an understanding of the theatricality of the restaurant business and how you and your partner will need to perform the many different roles of successfully putting up a production.
3. No restaurant owners except corporate owners discuss the costs or their ways of doing business but I'll share the dos and don'ts with you. Then we'll go through the process of opening our own make believe restaurant in New York City.

There is nothing harder than having a financially rewarding restaurant operation and a life with personal happiness that makes all the sacrifices and hard work worthwhile. There is no question that it's not easily done, but the pain and joy of my experiences definitely will help.

Think about it some more and if this is *what you want*, we'll proceed when you're ready.

A "Know What You Want" Exercise

Take a long walk, run or bike ride and announce to yourself that you have just won eight million Lotto dollars and only you know about it. Then tell yourself that all your money problems are gone for life and you never have to work for anyone again. Now take yourself on that dream trip you always fantasize about and when you feel like it, tell yourself you can do anything in the world you want. Now, what would you *want* that to be?

CHAPTER 2

The Mom and Pop way of doing it

2. The "Mom and Pop" Way of Doing It

If in your heart-of-hearts decision to pursue restaurant ownership you found yourself passionately determined to do what's necessary to succeed, you're to be congratulated because any effort short of that is doomed.

No matter what your life's restaurant experience has been or what your restaurant education is when you decide that one day you're going to be an owner, that's the day you need to start looking for a job. How do you like that idea? Not exactly what we want to hear when we're all wound up and ready to go. The collective we is you and I. Together we're going to purposefully plan, create and successfully own and operate our own restaurant.

So why would we need to get a job if we are going to open our own restaurant? Basically a well-known and widely used element of success is emulating the role model that got us thinking we could also be successful. Because no matter what we know and what we've learned about the restaurant business, it's not enough to role the dice and risk so much. The job we want for as long as it takes is any job we can get in the restaurant that excites and inspires us. The lessons to be learned feed into what we want to ultimately accomplish.

Wherever we choose to work and learn must be a successful owner operated business. We need access that allows us to observe and learn hands on from the operator about why and how he/she conducts business. This may take a little time, and might also take a few different places, but you'll never regret one moment. The experience will greatly enhance your personal resume and put a new spin on getting a job. There's nothing better than learning how things get done and learning how someone made something out of nothing. If this doesn't inspire us, it just becomes another job. But if the right choices are made now, when we're ready to do our own restaurant, the running of it will be the least of our worries.

Do you think someone out of a culinary school or a hotel restaurant school would or should work a summer at McDonalds? I do. Should they work in a family owned and operated Chinese or Italian restaurant, or an All American Steak and Seafood house? Any of them will do because they all have systems that work successfully. McDonalds feeds a tremendous number of people everyday of the year, all around the world. The quality is exact, the stores are clean and the people are friendly. That's unbelievable consistency, but understandable. The systems work and the business grows at a serious rate.

Family owned and operated restaurants do the same thing but they are much more specialized. Their systems work and they grow at their own desired pace. The Mom and Pop system can easily be understood and appreciated without going to Hamburger University.

In our new global world economy McDonalds thrives, as do many well-operated chain restaurants, while at the same time many similar operations are having problems. That's because the baby boomers now crossing the fifty-five yard line are changing their eating habits and, most importantly, where they want to eat.

Where the boomers want to eat is part of the changing landscape of the food industry. I'm a baby boomer myself and in my lifetime I've seen the restaurant industry go from my parent's type of place and their favorite Mom and Pop places to restaurants in strip malls and suburbs that gave way to chains in mega-malls which left Main Street America for dead.

The '80s also produced the jaded taste buds and appetites of the yuppies. Chefs became stars, prices skyrocketed, and rents left the bounds of reality at these new grazing palaces. In the meantime, the stock market crashed and corrected, and so has the restaurant business. Quality survived, but a lot of money and jobs disappeared. Consumers now dictate the appropriate menus and prices in different venues. Today's successful two-star restaurants, casual dining restaurants and fast food outlets are very much in touch with their consumers.

The people who know the products boomers are after are resurrecting Main Street America with their creative menus in smartly done makeovers that are well run by couples and teams that can remember names and make customers comfortable in the casual dining business of today and tomorrow.

Does this sound like the return to the Mom and Pop ways of doing it to you? You bet it is and it's a good business to be in. So let's spend a little time peeling the product onion and then we'll return to a further examination of the Mom and Pop ways of doing it.

What is Product in the restaurant business? It's the many components that add up to a successful customer experience. It's the greeting at the front door to a clean and pleasant atmosphere. And of course it's good food and value served by an interested and informed staff. Personable interaction with customers by the owner during their visit is of the utmost importance. And a sincere "thank you" upon their exit is mandatory. That is Product!

My favorite metaphor for the restaurant business is theater. And who has a better production playing to millions every day than McDonalds? Nobody! And doesn't our favorite restaurant do the same thing on a different scale. They both deliver their product day in and day out. That's systems working and professionalism. That's show business at its best. Product that delivers a feeling of satisfaction is the magic word. Product that makes you feel good is something very special.

Restaurants are theater? Yes! And you'll be surprised how closely related they are. The overriding working comparison is that restaurants and theaters are places where people gather to enjoy an experience that is not available in their private lives. It's where they and we socialize, enjoy life and friends, get stimulated and excited by new ideas or rediscover old ones. It's where we go to reward those we love and ourselves. It's where we go for romance and to move our hearts and souls for just a moment off the challenges and hard work of our daily lives.

No doubt about it, uplifting experiences are the music in our life's journey, and unique restaurants that satisfy our needs are never forgotten. Great theatrical experiences, whatever the format, concerts, sports events, movies, live shows, that expose us to the great talents of stars like Meatha, Everett, Pavarotti, Gibson, Streep, Baez, DeNiro, Pacino, Elvis, Marino, Montana, Mays, Mozart, Mantle, Griffey or Michael Jordan transport us to special places where we are enriched, excited and entertained, and where we always remember the experience.

I recently went out to dinner with my wife and her parents for a birthday celebration in upstate New York. It was a brand new restaurant owned by a well-known and respected owner. In the dead of winter from the moment we shook off the chill and entered the restaurant until we left, we had such an overwhelming good time that I'll always remember that night. It was so fine and we enjoyed each other and the occasion so much that even though my family tricked me out of the check, it was a great restaurant experience.

Later we'll visit this restaurant again because it is the Mom and Pop prototype of our dreams and why we all might want to do this. And on our return visit there, I'll get even in the check department.

How It Might Begin Or Planting The Seeds Of Commitment To This Business

When I was a kid I was like almost everyone I knew, just playing by the road of life waiting for those special days when my aunt or grandma who thought I was the greatest would take me away for the weekend. Sometimes my Aunt Sally would tell me to grab my cowboy boots and hat 'cause we were goin' to the National Rodeo where my uncle Billy, her son, was a star bronco rider.

I loved going to the Big Show. We always ate at great roadside food and truck stops where the cowgirls, truckers, cowboys, clowns and animal handlers ate. I had burgers bigger than my hat and my Aunt Sally always made sure my strawberry milk shake was double thick.

The rodeo scared the beejeezus out of me because I was only three and a half feet tall hangin' around back stage with my uncle Billy near the scary chutes of cowboys freaking out on the backs of livestock that were waiting to kill anybody on their backs or anybody walking on two feet. But it was exciting and the animals had a pretty good life style working six hours a week. They worked so hard at trying to kill cowboys that they all had the respect of anyone who worked around or on them.

After the rodeo was over Aunt Sally and I ate with all the rodeo personnel before they left for the next town. And believe me those rodeo promoters knew how to feed their people.

The meals that closed the show in each town were catered by local caterers. There were always white tablecloths and napkins set in a tent not fifty feet from the animals. I never remember saying goodbye to my uncle Billy or his wife Joanne or any of my rodeo friends because, shoot, I was dreaming in the back of Aunt Sally's 1947 Chevy by sundown. On the drive from Bakersfield or anywhere back to San Francisco late on a Sunday night, Aunt Sally would always wake me to split one last Wagon Wheel double thick strawberry shake before delivering me home.

So somehow the physical and psychological seeds of loving food and pleasant experiences with the theatrical rodeo show began to grow in the backfield of my mind. It's amazing because being around my parent's nightclub restaurant or my relative's places always filled me with dread.

At the age of six, I became the stable boy at Mack's Hitchrack. Everything changed when I began cleaning horse stables with my dog Daisy Mae. Mack told me women gardeners would pay for the horseshit if it was in bags and that he would split the dollar-a-bag with me. And he did! Some Saturdays I sold everything I bagged and Mack's wife

Eleanor fed Daisy Mae and me great hamburgers served on hot dog buns once we helped them clean up the restaurant after their Saturday lunch business. Then Mack would count the money. Well, he might have beaten me for a few bucks. I wouldn't have cared if I knew. But what he taught me was: "You can always make something out of nothing if you ain't afraid of shitty work!"

Mack and Eleanor were the quintessential Mom and Pop operators. They sent their kids to college and went through many ups and downs during their forty-two year run at the beach, but they were happy people who always made me laugh about anything that amused them in our horseshit business. They would claim my dog ate too many road apples or someone was stealing from me because inventory was down and maybe I should follow the horses with a lobby broom and bucket. Those moments were unforgettable and so were they.

Too soon, Mack died and Eleanor sold the real estate and took his ashes home to Ireland. The pooch and me were out of hamburgers and work. When we had it going Mack always pointed me home to pay my mom something. I'll never forget them or the inexpressible joy I felt as a kid when I split my Hitchrack pay with my mom.

Early on the seeds of commitment to the restaurant business were positively planted in my subconscious, and as I grew up I always found working in restaurants comfortable and satisfying. Maybe I could have gone to visit an uncle who was a beekeeper who taught me the science of the bees. Or maybe some one might have exposed me to the genius of Mozart and then maybe I might have been inspired to write *The Flight Of The Bronco Ridin' Bumble Bees*. Who knows when and where mentors will appear in our lives. In hindsight, I value Mack and Eleanor for appearing in mine.

I remember that they did it better than my own family. They had fun and loved each other and what they did.

A lot of things have changed in the world and the restaurant business since my introduction to it. I know that it's much harder and less familiar today, but those who succeed in the Mom and Pop Restaurant World enjoy what they do and who they do it with. The art of our lives is the work we do. When we do our work with the passion and discipline that uniquely defines our point of view in the restaurant business we will succeed.

CHAPTER 3

What are you bringing to the party?

3. What Are You Bringing to the Party?

When your restaurant work experience widens and you begin to have insight about how all the different departments work together and individually, your inner voice occasionally can be heard: "We can do this." There's nothing wrong with listening to that voice but keeping it in check is the rule for now. There will be a big click with a burning white light when we are absolutely consumed and prepared well enough to be the creator/producer of our own little world. Until that time we have to be very clear and honest with ourselves.

On a good day we should sit down with pen and paper and look at our strengths and weaknesses. How can we guide our dreams and desires to the drawing board where we're going to be the creators unless we know our limitations and how close we can get to pulling it off?

I read somewhere that the most powerful tool in business today is a blank piece of paper. If you fill the paper with creative ideas, goals and disciplined do-able plans to make an idea work, you're in the better business ballpark. Before we jump in we should know what we can bring to the game. Let's start with our weaknesses.

Weak Restaurant Operational Skills

Here's are some thoughts about what I consider to be serious weaknesses in the operational skills necessary to run a restaurant:

1. I don't know anything about doing bookwork.
2. I really dislike waiting on people.
3. I never learned about ordering liquor or monitoring bar costs.
4. I can't even ask my own family for money, let alone strangers.

5. I've never been in trouble so I don't know any good attorneys or tax accountants.
6. I hate saying no to people and I hate confrontations.
7. I know about sales tax but I don't know about corporation taxes.
8. I know about fire insurance but not liquor liability insurance.
9. I just learned that banks don't make loans to restaurants and restaurant equipment people only take cash.
10. I can't do hiring and firing.

Strong Restaurant Operational Skills

On the positive side, here are some strengths people can capitalize on that are critical to the smooth operation of a restaurant:

1. I can run the back of the house where I work. I can order and receive foods, produce, dry goods, fish and cleaning supplies.
2. I like the back of the house. My controls keep our food cost around 30%. I've set a trap for a guy I believe is stealing from us.
3. I can cook breakfast and can handle the big lunch rush.
4. Burgers are my deal. One day I want to own my own chain of burger houses. I call them "The Eight Wonders Of The World."
5. I created the "Wonder Burger." It's a grilled meatloaf burger with melted cheese and grilled onions on top. I serve it on a sour dough roll.
6. If it's broken I can fix it.
7. I can't stand filth or dirty uniforms. I say you are what you look like.
8. I like my co-workers. We all like having lunch after lunchtime business with our owner boss and talking about new menu ideas we have for the kitchen.
9. I want that kitchen because I would and could make it better. I'd stay open for dinner.

10. I have never raised my voice to any of the wait staff. I do not smoke or curse too much and when I can I try to learn the bar from the owner. Sometimes he lets me do the slow lunches behind the bar.

How close would we be if we were the above? If you said "not within light years," I would understand. But what if we could find that guy/gal for the back of the house in a new venture? I'd give him/her a lot to know we had the back of the house covered and locked up. If you're in a different restaurant experience world with more to bring to the party that's great, but hopefully you'll take the time to perform this lesson because I'm certain you can see the simple beauty of this tool.

For just an hour of your time you can begin to look at the big picture of the little world we want to create. You can see your shortcomings and what you need to learn. You can know, own and improve your strengths and skills. Until we have all the required skills and knowledge, we are understudies learning all the time. Every job we take to learn the required skills takes us closer to the lead part.

Suppose the previous exercise was an accurate assessment of our acquired skills. How would we proceed? What I come away with from this exercise is a profile of a young man or woman with great energy and enthusiasm. The young man or woman also possesses a love for the business, has learned how to run the back of the house and still has the desire to learn it all.

Such a person with a great work ethic and the dream to be an owner-operator has great potential for success in this business. What they lack are the studied skills of running the front of the house and office and the ability to merge all these different elements into a functioning restaurant. Young people need the time and experiences that help develop these skills and shape their personalities for this people-oriented profession.

I would proceed with learning right away about the legal paper work required in the restaurant business. I'd ask my boss to let me help in the office chores one afternoon a week at no charge. I'd ask about payables and how credit card charges work. I'd take a few classes in restaurant management at trade schools and send away for information that I felt pertinent at this time. Two very useful and informative sources of reading materials specifically tailored for anyone serious about entering the restaurant business are:

1. *Guide to Restaurants and Bars*
   Practitioners Publishing Company
   1-800-323-8724
   I found about this book because it was mainly written for accountants. Our accountant had it on his bookshelf and I couldn't stop looking at it. It cost about $150.00 but is well worth every penny. (If your accountant isn't familiar with this publication I'd re-think that situation.)

2. The Library of the National Restaurant Association
   1-800-424-5156
   As their catalog states, they offer all the current information that you need to run a successful food-service operation. Again, well worth every penny. These are "must have" reference materials.

Learning is doing. It doesn't matter if you're attending an expensive culinary school or a trade school, or you're working in a restaurant you like. You're learning to always keep your eyes on the prize.

Where do you want to be in two, three and five years? When you hear that voice talking to you, find the time, paper and pen and get in touch with who you are and what you can bring to the party.

Always keep in mind that all professionals candidly and astutely monitor their progress and focus on their goals. That's how it works.

When you define where you need your operational skills to be, like we've defined on the following page, it demonstrates you're going to hear the big click and see the burning white light.

Where Our Operational Skills Need To Be

1. I can read and understand monthly bookkeeping reports but sometimes the bookkeeper says I'm too compulsive about every penny.
2. Waiting on people is a job that takes one good line in a greeting to free them up to enjoy what we do and for me to control the situation. I worry about repeating myself.
3. I can pour a twenty five hundred dollar bar on a busy summer night and run a real tight pour cost, but I'm not selling fine wines.
4. I'm all over the place and I know our customers. They know me and what I want to do in the future and they give me their cards that I file and note. I still feel uncomfortable telling them what a share in my make believe restaurant is going to cost. It's not the amount. It's just awkward.
5. Accountants and lawyers don't annoy me, their bills do. I really dislike doctors and dentists even more but this is part of the big picture of doing business in the real world.
6. Saying no to customers doesn't bother me in the least. We do a great job and if that isn't enough they can go elsewhere. But I do have angst over wondering and second-guessing ourselves if anyone ever would leave.
7. I have a working class attitude about taxes so every week I deposit a prorated tax amount into a tax account. I hate that saying "the only two things you can be sure of in this life are death and taxes," because it's true.

8. We use one insurance company's wrap-around policy. Three months before it expires we shop it. It's all-inclusive and always seems expensive to me. I have problems with that so now I do the shopping around of the policy.
9. Banks are very frustrating institutions to deal with. We use different ones for different options that benefit the restaurant. My attitude now is neither borrower nor lender be at the banks.
10. Sometimes day and night I look at my watch and realize that time does fly and the only thing that's ever going to buy me time is the hiring of the right person and the firing of the wrong ones. Still though I worry about being sued for violating someone's something. You know what I mean?

The Restaurant Strengths Of Our Partnership

1. I started in the back of the house where I currently work and I learned a lot about ordering and receiving goods. As time went by I became a better-educated buyer and a more demanding cut-throat customer. I formed relationships with vendors that serve us well and provided us with the best product at the best price. I learned that compromise here is deadly. Our quality is demanding. Our standards are well known. And we will not accept anything less. We believe you should get what you pay for.
2. Food costs vary, as do the seasons and our customers. What doesn't vary is the acceptable bottom line food cost of our restaurant. Our kitchen must maintain a food cost controlled menu, seasonal or otherwise, and a payroll that is in sync with our budget for the back of the house.
3. I still cook but now prefer the front of the house. When I think about my own restaurant I see myself running a small but tight ship, and like my current boss, I want to be attentive to the customer. I can't do that from the kitchen.

4. I'm a long way from my hamburger dreams, though that was a great idea that I might do someday. What I want to do now is my own restaurant. I've got a line on an existing small place in an area that's growing. It's a situation that I can handle financially by myself with my savings next year. My boss has been helping me with the business plan and is giving me a lot of support. He thinks it's the right move at the right time. I want to do a checkered tablecloth Italian restaurant in a neighborhood where there's everything but good Italian food.
5. My friend Paolo has committed to come in with me. He's the only guy I'd do a Northern Italian restaurant with because he spent two years training in Tuscany. We've done the menu, food costs, equipment costs and kitchen overhead expenses. It works in our minds and on paper and we're excited.
6. Together we'll do all the improvements. No building permits are required. We're getting three months rent-free from the landlord for the make over and a five-year lease with a second five-year option. The Doing Business As (DBA) is "Tusculum."
7. We've priced out insurance. We've found an accountant and an attorney that handles liquor licenses. If we're smart and handle it right away we'll have a beer and wine license for opening night.
8. Paolo and I are meeting with different purveyors and wine distributors. Twice a week we test try breads, menu items and wines.
9. We decide to expose the kitchen. Paolo, his help and our kitchen will be on display. I like the cleanliness requirement that it puts on our staff and us.
10. Paolo has two people on his payroll and I have two people. To start, we're only open for dinner six nights a week, five hours a night. When needed, we'll do more. For now, that's what we're comfortable with, assuming our projections are accurate.

I'd say these guys are ready to go. What gets me excited about their project is that they've kept it simple. It's within their budget and a great Mom and Pop starter project. It's in a growing neighborhood where they've done their homework, planning, projections, market testing and research.

Most importantly, we can see in the second exercise where the working in a restaurant that inspires and excites you is time well spent. The experience gained clearly shows. If we wanted to get picky, we could find some faults but I'd say they're coming to the party prepared and the point is well made: Without a well rounded, hands-on restaurant background and a personal assessment of where we are and where we want to get, we're lost and we'll never hear the big click or see the burning white light!

This is the time and place where you, the reader, become Paolo in the collective "We" we're using. This way you'll be learning as a doer in the exercises that follow. But be forewarned and reread the plaque, because when the party's over in this business you don't just turn out the lights and go home!

I was once picking up a piece of equipment I thought I bought from a successful New York City restaurant owner named Pauley. Pauley tried to open a restaurant in the theater district and for a variety of reasons, he went under. Like a shrewd survivalist dressed in weasel fur, he brought in an auctioneer and tried to escape with any money he could before the landlord changed the locks and the purveyors and sales tax people showed up. My helper and I almost had moved the ice machine out the back door when a scared Pauley climbed over us and said: "If you're smart, you'll follow me NOW!"

I squeezed back into the empty restaurant and went to get my tools when I heard another voice say, "I know you're in there Pauley! You owe me sixteen big in fish, so pay me now or I'll show you how you're gonna pay later tonight at your uptown dump. You've got one minute pal. Don't continue to disappoint us!"

I thought they were going to shoot up the place, so I hurried back towards the ice machine. All of a sudden, the whole front of the restaurant started collapsing as a garbage truck backed ten feet into the room. I threw my tools to my helper and squeezed past the back of the ice machine in the doorway and saw for the first time in big bold print: WARNING THIS MACHINE LEASED BY ACME REFRIGERATION. BRONX, N.Y.

I lost the money I'd spent at auction on an ice machine I thought was owned by Pauley who owned the restaurant. This jerk Pauley almost got us seriously hurt because the last words I heard as we left the space were: "If my f—in' ice machine ain't here Pauley, you's gonna get neutered!"

At the end of the back alley entrance to the restaurant other weasels had Pauley trapped. He was groveling and paying up. I'd bet the bank that everybody owed money got it back from Pauley with interest for their trouble because both he and his successful uptown place never got neutered and his garbage was picked up. He paid me back every dime and apologized with a dinner.

Basically it was just another restaurant wake up call in the big city that got filed under Things To Not Do. Always be aware that the restaurant business has a slimy underbelly that makes a great deal of money off the mistakes and naiveté of those with the money but without The Know How! We all have fantasies about heroes, money, love, sex, and success but fantasies about this business without the required necessary skills can quickly turn lives into nightmares.

I know a soda systems executive that sets up restaurants big and small. And he's no different from the computer systems guy, the credit card company guy or any businessman that has leased property at risk in the restaurant business. They don't want to find out that their expensive equipment was lost in a sneaky quick auction like Pauley's before they can legally get it back. When you talk to these guys about these kinds of things, they all say the same thing: "Most people don't have a clue about the restaurant business anymore so we get their money up front. We hog-tie them legally on leases made by different finance companies we hire to be worse than pit bulls. When they realize they don't know what they're doing in the restaurant business and they're about to get buried alive by debt, they get desperate. Desperate people do stupid things."

Aside from bogus insurance claims for faked robberies, and owner-started fires, many other stupid things take place when money is owed. The blame for failure is a tough bullet to dodge. Enough said! I could beat this to death like a rented car but the point is simply:

The restaurant business is very complex and complicated. If you're not bringing the required skills and the necessary experience to the party, you can bet that the effort will turn into a painful, expensive and sometimes dangerous failure.

CHAPTER 4

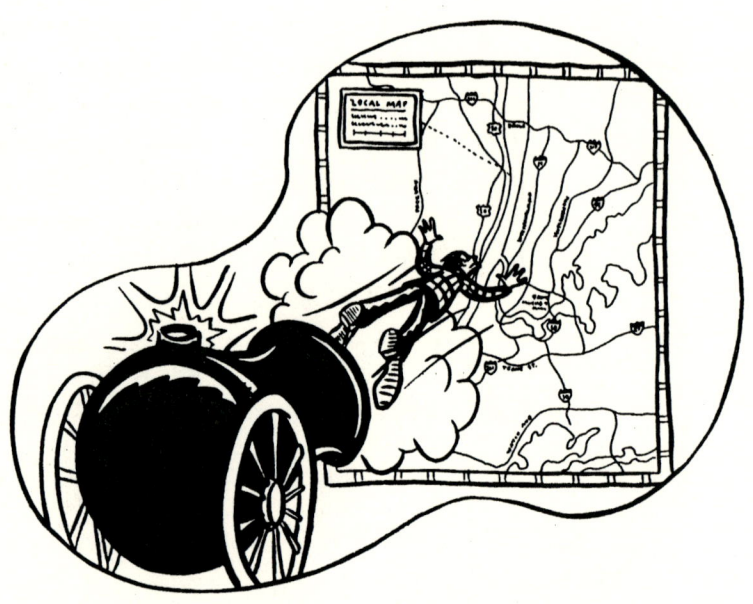

LOCATION...LOCATION...LOCATION

4. Location. Location. Location.

The name of the restaurant game is the same as the real estate game: *Location. Location. Location. Baby!*

I've never screwed up anything that hurt more than learning the accuracy of this cliché. In the previous chapters we focused on the personal preparation needed to make it to the Big Time and the critical preparation of one's self. Committing yourself and your assets to finding a place to buy or rent for business is the Next Big Step.

Where are we going to do what we've worked so hard to prepare to do? It doesn't matter if you're Wolfgang Puck looking for the next Spago location or McDonalds walking away from a location that did not work out. We all want the same thing: *the site that best attracts our customers.* As this lesson will illustrate, finding and selecting a restaurant location is decidedly the most important decision we'll make in the process of opening a restaurant. We'll examine the many considerations of this task after I share with you a story that illustrates all the mistakes I made once in the big city.

My N.Y.C. Story, Part 1

EATING THE BIG ONE!

I came to New York in 1980 and enrolled in graduate school. I supported myself by working in a big restaurant as an expediter in the back of the house. I took food orders from the waiters and waitresses and relayed the orders to the various cooks who made the meals. The kitchen was huge and the volume of food served daily was staggering.

My job kept the chaos somewhat under control, but it was nerve-racking and hard to work with so many diverse personalities.

At the end of a shift a bunch of us would unwind and have some beers at another place. One night after work and some beers, I was walking home on the Upper West Side and noticed that a restaurant that had just opened that evening was still doing business around midnight. There's nothing unusual about that except that they only served one item, grilled chicken, and they were doing serious business.

Like any curious restaurant spy I walked in, checked it out and left with a whole grilled chicken, pita bread and salsa in less than three minutes. The chicken was excellent and very similar to the Pollo Loco chicken that I knew from Southern California. I never thought much more about it, but I did eat a lot of that chicken over the next year and I thoroughly enjoyed it.

Oddly enough, one night a bunch of friends and I were on an uptown east side train going to a party. We got off in the eighties. Coming up the stairs to the street I could smell the unmistakable smell of my favorite chicken. The nose always knows.

There on a busy prime city corner was the exact same chicken store from the west side having its grand opening this very evening. The owner's face lit up when he saw all my friends and me get on line for a snack. He didn't charge us for anything, saying I was his number one customer. Everyone loved his or her chicken and I told him so as we were leaving. I also told him I thought he had a great idea in a good place. Then I heard the following: Location. Location. Location. Baby!

I haven't a clue as to why I asked him if he had more stores planned or why I told him I was interested, but I did.

He laughed and said we'd talk about it sometime. I excitedly talked about it all night with my pals at the party we went to. Later that night I must have bumped my head because the next day I was talking to Mister Chicken.

Guess what happened?

The guy told me he was so busy that he'd offer me a deal on his next uptown store if I would come up with something like a franchise fee, co-sign the lease and cover startup expenses. I must have done more than bumped my head because I accepted. Fifteen minutes later I'm standing with Mister Chicken on the corner of 102nd Street and Madison Avenue in front of the new store.

Rush hour traffic is very heavy on Madison and the shift change at Mount Sinai Hospital fills the sidewalks with hundreds of bodies. I'm smiling. Mister Chicken is smiling and saying: Location. Location. Location. Baby!

"Absolutely man," I say in agreement, nodding because the bump on my head is making me feel just like Ray Kroc must have felt when he went into business with the McDonald brothers. I didn't see chickens flying out of my store, I saw millions of dollar bills flying in the front door.

The glaring oversight on my part was that I didn't even notice the Warning Plaque. I had no guidelines and no frame of reference on what to look for. I wasn't finding out any critical data from Mister Chicken or anyone else. I learned later that the private clinic above the store wasn't a Health Clinic, it was a Methadone Clinic that opened in the early morning hours to dispense medication and closed at three in the afternoon. This timing gave the junkies that I was ignoring a great hustle: get your stuff and prescriptions for free, sell them and get the real stuff. I paid no attention to the threatening, toothless, slow moving humans showing me their stashes in hands the size of baseball gloves as they mumbled the menu prices.

No. There I was an experienced restaurant person stupidly and excitedly thinking I'm Ray Kroc. I was letting my greed and delusions of grandeur blind me from the sleight of hand Mister Chicken was pulling. He was expertly off-loading a bad location into my waiting hands.

I didn't pay attention to the fact that none of the evening Mount Sinai shift wouldn't cross 102nd from 101st because of the junkies. Nor did I notice that the East Harlem Projects were just waking up and walking down the block in large numbers to Church's Fried Chicken on the next corner where all business was conducted through bank-style bulletproof windows protected by an armed security guard. And I refused to see that all the car traffic raced through the Projects and wouldn't stop at traffic lights because of the junkies.

Suffice it to say that the next six months of my life were the worst! Just how humiliating and painful can eating the big one be? Try handing out flyers on the corner across the street from your empty store that's going down as quickly as the tossed flyers blow down the street to the feet of the hustling junkies who are conducting their business in front of your business. It's the end of the world as you know it.

* * *

What really happened on 102nd Street? By the time it was over I had lost everything. All gone. I ate the big one without ever giving a thought to what I really wanted. My big mistake wasn't being hustled and hung out to dry in the wrong "location, location, location, baby." It was the lack of honesty with myself about my abilities and expertise.

Just because I had worked in restaurants my whole life did not mean I was qualified and prepared to go into the business. Wait staff, cooks, bartenders and hostesses *do not* qualify as restaurateurs. I certainly didn't. I simply didn't know what I wanted and I didn't know what I was doing. People who know what they want know exactly where they're going. They make a science project out of choosing a location. They don't make it an art project or a money making fantasy. They are drop dead serious and they do their homework thoroughly.

My personal debts ran on and accrued interest for years for money owed to former loved ones, friends and the never relenting state and federal tax people. I worked for years to pay those debts back because I felt if I didn't pay them, I'd never forget how I acquired them. It still bothers me to this day that every one of those paid back friendly investors has never said thanks or hello. That's because when we hustle up funds from friends and loved ones they invest in us, and if we fail them, human nature chimes in and changes those relationships where money is and was involved. It's sad but true. The cost of doing business with friends and family is very high and should be avoided at all times.

When we are really ready to go and we know *what* we're looking for, we'll go to different areas looking for the right location. We'll search with a list clipped to our clipboard that includes standards and requirements such as:

1. Who and where are our customers in this area?
2. How does the competition rate in this area?
3. What's available within our budget and game plan?
4. What's in the restaurant graveyard (un-rented or empty restaurant spaces) here or nearby?
5. What does any prospective location have going for it that serves our concept?
6. What are the restrictions and limitations of a potential site?

Simple enough, right? Hardly! If this is the most important decision we'll make in our effort to go into business I'd say we need to know more. We clearly know what's at risk and to make the downside more manageable let's break it down further.

At this stage of pre-production we should focus on our audience/customer. We should realistically ask ourselves if the audience/customer base in this area is more than large enough to make our restaurant work:

7. Are we in an area that people live in or are we in a situation that requires people to travel to us?

8. Is it a residential neighborhood type of location or a destination type of location? There's a big difference in cities from one section to the next and Main Street rents are greater than side street rents.
9. Will we be able to find the type of people we want to work for us in this area?
10. Does the area lend itself to a steady year round customer base we can draw from all year or is it a seasonal location?
11. Are our potential customers in this area in the morning only?
12. Do they lunch where they work?
13. Do they dine out in this area when they return home or do they go elsewhere?

Who And Where Are Our Customers?

We've decided that we want to do a fifty to sixty seat Mom and Pop style restaurant in the city where we live because we intimately know our neighborhood. It's on the upper West side, which has a population of young and very dollar/value conscious inhabitants. It's also a strong, year-round population that dines out daily. When the population goes to work elsewhere, another population comes to work in the neighborhood.

Nearby museums, galleries, and high-end shopping areas also draw a lunching and dining population to the area every day. That's who the customer is and where they are. It's also why the rents are astounding.

How Does The Competition Rate Around the Area?

Staying with the Mom and Pop style establishment and the concept mentioned earlier, a Northern Italian fifty to sixty seat restaurant, our concept is to bring back the simple neighborhood operation we grew up appreciating and enjoying. During my time in New York I again experienced what I knew from growing up in San Francisco. I sought out these restaurants and began to notice they were getting harder to find. It's sad to report this, but the Mom and Pop places that offered so many different cuisines are rapidly disappearing.

Once I asked a guy who owned a great little place in Little Italy if he was going to sell to the Chinese who were slowly expanding Chinatown across Canal Street into Little Italy. He said, "What can I do? My kids are Long Island kids. Cars, boys, girls and colleges! Forgetta 'bout it! They don't come to the city unless Springsteen's playing the Garden. They don't work, they play."

So in the late '80s, high-end pasta places started popping up all over New York. A lot of schmoozing, euro-designed and stylish operators made it work. Landlords loved it, rents went crazy and pasta got very pricey. A former space of mine in New York that had a rent of $3000 a month in 1985 is getting $16,000 a month in 2000. Granted, it's a prime location, but few can afford it and neither can all those pasta palaces anymore. So the fad restaurants get bumped, and the next restaurant production makeover begins.

In our exercise we're going to concentrate on finding a side street location that will be recognized soon enough by our targeted audience. When you live in a neighborhood, you always watch with great interest what comes and goes in your neighborhood. Our competition on the upper West side, quite frankly, died five to ten years ago.

Now the area is littered with pizza parlors serving bad pasta. Within our ten square block high-density neighborhood, there is not one Mom and Pop style restaurant surviving in today's real estate market. If we find the right, affordable location, we'll be the only ones producing our type of product and production for a potentially large and appreciative audience.

Another spin on the competition is that if it exists, it can bring out the best in us and what we do. For example, where my current business is located, there are restaurants always coming and going. But the good ones stay and that's the way it should be.

I also firmly believe that any good business in our town whether it's a restaurant or another business, is good for our business. Good businesses draw people to our town and positively charge the whole local economy.

A friend of mine who owns a nearby restaurant views competition very differently. He just rented the space next to his so no one could feed off or compete with his business. He plans to cover the expenses with catering and seasonal brunches.

If competition is an issue in our location search, it can be evaluated by patronizing any and all competitors on weeknights and, especially, weekends. We'll learn right away if the competitors are killing each other or if there is plenty of room in the market for us to succeed.

What's Available Within Our Budget And Game Plan?

We'll know the answer after we walk every block of the Upper West Side and talk to different realtors. Let everyone of them you make contact with know who you are, what you're looking for and vaguely what your budget is. Never negotiate any deal in the restaurant business with your real budget. Realtors can be very helpful and if any fees are involved, we'll get them factored into the deal later on, but use their information and their skills. Take their cards and call them daily. Very quickly you'll find a couple of good ones that you can relate to and who understand your needs.

The last page in the Money and Business section of the Sunday New York Times, under the heading Business Opportunities and Restaurants For Sale, is my favorite source of what's on the market in the city. Until this day, even though I'm no longer in the city, I check this page every week. Use comparable listings in other regions of the country. Pay no attention to asking prices, but do pay attention to addresses. Sift through the lies, half-truths and over valued fire sales like a vulture, because we're never going to be interested in buying or paying top dollar for someone else's failure.

This kind of cold-blooded research in the restaurant graveyard will begin to give us an understanding of the restaurant market. We'll start to have a sense of what can be done within our budget and what it costs when "location, location, location" mistakes are made.

What's In The Restaurant Graveyard Here Or Nearby?

Because we've decided that our restaurant is going to be in the city, it's to our advantage to acquaint ourselves with the out-of-business and vacant restaurant spaces in our chosen area. Walking each block can certainly be time well spent, depending on several factors:

1. If the specific location of the failed restaurant is lousy, it won't matter if the rent is cheap and the place is fully equipped.
2. What the people in the neighborhood tell you. Try and find out about the store's history and problems.
3. The history of the place. Sometimes terrible locations are snake-bit. Businesses continue to come into these places, put tons of money and work into the stores, and people just won't go there. People are suspect of certain places that have had shaky pasts and a history of failure.
4. Will we be paying for other people's mistakes or garbage? Often the landlord is stuck for back rents and evicts the tenant. The landlord then takes possession of the contents of his abandoned restaurant space, which he'll try to pass onto the next renter as a fixture fee. I recently went through this while looking at a potential site. It was a pretty decent location but formerly a Chinese restaurant. Consequently, the interior design was terrible for our purposes. The equipment was completely shot and of no use to us. Lots of candy stoves and wok stations, not to

mention the filth of twenty years of frying foods. Yet the landlord was asking a hefty upfront fixture fee. I very calmly, but firmly, gave him some words to live by for trying to sell me garbage. Two weeks later he got what he wanted and workers were gutting the place for the next victim.

5. What does any prospective location have going for it that serves our concept? Does the space have any interesting design aspects that would make our concept work? Maybe there are windows that have a certain charm or a storefront that will be a warm welcome after we paint it. Maybe the equipment suits our needs and can be gotten at the right price. Maybe the dropped ceiling can be removed and there's a tin ceiling waiting to be brought back to life. Maybe just sitting across the street looking at the site gives us the right vibe or feeling. Do we somehow know it's the right place, in the right spot, at the right price?

6. What are the restrictions and limitations of a potential site? These two words are deal killers and we should be very clear about what they can be and how they could apply to our potential choices.

Restrictions—The one person who can be the biggest help in informing us of restrictions is the city, town or county building inspector. Ask for their help because they're normally very willing to give you some guidance, but never try to get one over on them, If you do and proceed without their blessings, advice and permits, they'll bury you and the project. Other restrictions include:

- We can have the best site visibility and access to millions of people only to find that the zoning has changed and the area is no longer a commercial area. The property's Grandfather Clause can expire, reverting back to the original residential-usage zoning.
- Insufficient parking space for the Health Department formulas.

- The septic may need to be upgraded to a water treatment plant because of new laws.
- Local zoning restricts expansion without site plan review and open hearings. Everything must be stamped and approved by licensed professionals and lawyers. It's *unbelievable* what has to be done today to start a business. It's very expensive.

Limitations—These are also very disheartening when starting a business, especially when they surprise you. I knew two guys in the city that paid for a space for a bar and grill. They started working away on building it, only to be turned down for a liquor license because they were within two hundred feet of the back door to an elementary school. They lost serious money by trying to save money in hiring a friend that was a lawyer instead of a liquor attorney.

- People who live above a restaurant complain all the time, calling agencies about odors and noises.
- Landlords can be very sneaky with the dos and don'ts of a restaurant lease. Across the board, any and all changes we request or have to make will cost extra unless this is all straightened out before any signing is done. Leases are where real estate attorneys earn their money.
- A change in the seating capacity of a restaurant can potentially impact the Fire Department's requirements for our space. For example, I filed plans for a two hundred square foot addition to my restaurant and was informed by our engineer that the state has a new sprinkler law that's being enforced this year when a space seats more than one hundred people. Aside from the tremendous expense of installing sprinklers, there are additional exit alterations required, resulting in substantial improvement and insurance costs. The same goes for the Health Department. Their demands for changes in kitchens, bathrooms, parking, sep-

tic and sanitation add considerable, and sometimes incredible, costs to a project.

Can we do it? Absolutely. But paying attention to all the pre-production details is where the whole project succeeds or fails. It's like the old baseball saying, "The best pitch in baseball is strike one."

CHAPTER 5

What to do right...right away...
to avoid the Big One!

5. What to Do Right Away to Avoid the Big One!

If we have succeeded in getting the point across, which is to understand and be aware of the risk and skill required to select a suitable site, the big picture begins to take shape and the theater analogy becomes applicable. Now that we're out looking at locations in a specific area and price range, we are very much like producers looking for the theater to house their production. Just like a theatrical producer, we're looking for the best situation to create a world in which we have complete control over every detail.

Empty theaters, like empty restaurants, are waiting for the next show to be staged. The great shows have long lives and great financial rewards. When it's over, they pack out and the next production takes over, changes the set, cast and crew. Up goes the curtain and the play begins. The paying audience continues to come as long as they're not disappointed, and the critics approve and appreciate the production. If this perspective is understood and our understanding translates into the realities of creating something out of nothing, we're on our way.

Get organized right away by considering what we need to do to stay a few steps head of our competitors:

1. Before getting emotionally involved with a site, a partner or investors, get your thoughts organized and seek counsel. The best lawyer that can understand and advise you in the task ahead is an experienced liquor license attorney. They've pretty much seen and heard it all. They seem to know everyone in the business. Through their connections, information and names can be relayed to save you time and money.

2. Find out about informative restaurant publications and textbooks from which we can begin to formulate our strategies.
3. Narrow our choices to three strong possibilities through continued neighborhood searches. Then get or make floor plans of these spaces and begin to put our ideas into the floor plans to find out what does or doesn't work.
4. Choose our real estate attorney and use our real estate contacts for lease details about these spaces.
5. Start making trips to our restaurant equipment district and learn about prices on everything we think we'll need. A walk around to meet different sellers is a money saving exercise that will really surprise you.
6. Continue our visits to different operators in our chosen area and learn about what they do well or not so well. In fact we do become restaurant spies—and very observant ones. It's great to learn about things that different operators do well or poorly. But a word of caution: *Loose lips sink ships.* Do not share our ideas, plans or hopes with others. It's an energy waster and can cause (or create) problems.
7. Start thinking in dollars and *sense*. If we don't yet think the restaurant business is high risk, visit a bank for a startup loan to make us believers. The fact is, banks do not loan money for startup restaurants. The government, through The Small Business Administration, won't even loan money for restaurant ventures. It comes from either others or us.

What kind of money situation can we live with? The best one includes enough of our own money; the second best is to take on partners or investors.

Thinking about money is tricky. People will talk about many personal details of their lives, but never about their money, because it's a real touchy subject. If we can, we want to avoid using anybody's money but our own. Maybe we're a year away from doing this with what money we have available. If we have enough money to handle the first year of fixed business expenses we're as ready now as we're ever going to be.

But before we spend one dime, we're going to get some free expert advice and estimates. From who do you think? These people, who are likely to dispense free advice every day:

1. The area's Building Inspector who will tell us what needs to be done to open or re-open this space as a restaurant.
2. The Health Department officials who will tell us what we need to do to comply with the latest regulations.
3. Any relative or friend that is an expert or professional in the areas of construction. It probably won't cost more than a few drinks and meals after we open. Free help can save hundreds and possibly thousands of dollars in renovation costs, whether electrical, plumbing, heating and air conditioning, or finish work.
4. Make friends with your new neighbors. Weed out the useless ones and use the help offered by the good ones. We're in it to win it and that's politically correct and smart business.

We'll also need important advice from a couple of paid experts:

• The aforementioned attorneys to whom we pay fees for educated opinions.
• A registered engineer who can tell us if we have any hidden structural problems at the different sites.

My N.Y.C. Story, Part 2

LEAVING EAST HARLEM AND MISTER CHICKEN.

I'm trying in this exercise to be so much more than I was when the chicken place closed, but it's like Method Acting. If you think back to a strong emotional experience of your past, you can easily bring it back and use the emotions to take you through a scene's emotional requirements. But as I type these words, it all comes back so quickly, like the way a smell or a musical note can take you back. It's definitely not easy looking back at where you lost unless you can file the loss in your learning experience folder and learn from it.

I was so angry at being duped and losing everything I had borrowed that I scared Mister Chicken into giving me back my lease-rent security deposit. I emptied the empty chicken restaurant of all my stuff and drove my beater car across town. New York City, the town without pity, was sound asleep as I waited at the red light on 86th Street and Columbus Avenue to make a left turn. It was raining and red flashing lights two blocks away reflected in the windows of shops and puddles.

I made my turn and a young cop at the corner of 84th and Columbus said I couldn't go any further. I couldn't make a left turn and head up the street to my apartment because there were cops everywhere, all over the place. I parked the beast and went into the corner deli.

Rick, my morning coffee counter friend, was just starting his workday and loving the drama all around him. He told me that the guy next door, the owner of this weird bar and night club had gotten out of a gypsy cab that was waiting on him to go get some money and pay his fare. But instead of paying his fare he fired two shotgun blasts at the cabby. He missed, but still caused a lot of damage because the cab hit other cars and the deli. Any resident of this pocket of the Upper West side knew that Mr. J ran numbers and dope out of his illegal club and that he was a big user himself.

Columbus Avenue from 79th up to 86th, in the late seventies and early eighties was the all time record holder for homicides. On one block within a twelve hour time span, ten dead bodies were picked up in drug related deaths out of burned out and boarded up buildings called "the Tombs" (80th to 81st between Columbus and Amsterdam Avenues).

I went outside with a beer in a bag and looked at all these cops and their weapons waiting to get Mr. J. out of his place. Most of the cops were joking around in their SWAT outfits that Mr. J probably nodded off and that Joy Boy Roy Rogers should go get him. Joy Boy Roy Rogers was the name these cops used for a wacky horse-riding cop in the neighborhood. With $5000 cash in my pockets, I felt safe surrounded by all this might. Little did I know that, as Joy Boy Roy Rogers entered the club on his horse and dragged the roped Mr. J out, the CLICK I was hearing was telling me what $5000 and a dream could do with this space.

Remember when I mentioned that in the city everyone notices a change in his or her neighborhood? I had been noticing a lot of changes just like any other local resident, but when I saw the Tombs being turned into condos three blocks away and witnessed the demise of Mr. J's club, an idea I had started making noises in my head.

The landlord of the corner building that housed Mr. J's and the deli on Columbus Avenue appeared to check up on what all his tenants in the building were freaking out about. This slumlord bully was a jerk. He sucker punched Mr. J for not paying rent as the cops were taking him away in handcuffs. The slumlord's assistant watched him and snickered as the guy ranted and raved, making an ass out of himself. He told me: "That's why everyone, even his own kids hate him!" The guy told me this in the midst of all the craziness we were watching. I turned to this perfect stranger and said: "I want to rent this place. I've got a great idea!"

The guy, Hal, shook my hand and gave me his phone number, telling me not to bother with Leon the owner. Instead, he'd mention me to

Leon's mother who thought Leon was an idiot for renting to the likes of Mr. J.

I called Hal and we met the next day for coffee. The upshot of our meeting was that if I agreed to take care of him to the tune of one thousand dollars after the signing of the lease, he'd make sure I got the lease. Evidently, Leon's mother trusted Hal's opinions and judgments and then she would tell Leon what she wanted done. Hal also cautioned me about Leon's devious ways of doing business and told me to never appear too eager around him when they were together and Leon was playing Mr. Big. We shook on the deal and his last words were, "Leon's a fool for compliments. You'll see!"

I trusted my instincts about Hal and after about three months of a lot of stupid things, I had a five-year lease with a second five-year option in my hands.

Oh yeah, I paid Hal his thousand dollars and had to give Leon two thousand cash and let him think that I thought he was a great guy. But I got a lease below market value, four free months of rent to fix the place up and a monthly rent of one thousand dollars until we opened for business. All my money was gone and I was back working in a restaurant to survive, but as I walked down the streets with that lease in my hands I kept repeating one word, "*Fishbones. Fishbones.* It'll be called *Fishbones!*"

CHAPTER 6

The Business Plan

6. The Business Plan

If you fail to plan, you are planning to fail. That's a wake up call. Never forget that catchy little pearl of wisdom because it's so true. This chore is a 'must-be-done-now' task. We've got confidence in our skills. We've got some money. We're willing to do the hard work. We're lining up places and people who'll help us get it done. All of this is based on assuming our idea can't fail. But assuming is lame. Very few unplanned endeavors win. (Note: The National Restaurant Association, 1-800-482-9122, can send you: *A Guide To Preparing A Restaurant Business Plan* #CS311.)

Creating The Operating And Business Plan

Here are a few of the things we need to do to create our operating and business plan:

1. Trademark our chosen name "The Tusculum Ristorante"
2. Have our accountant file with the IRS so we get our Employers Identification Number (EIN).
3. Be ready to file for a liquor license.
4. Get the Health Department Permit.
5. Secure the appropriate insurance coverage.
6. Select a neighborhood bank to do business with.
7. Develop or adopt an in-house bookkeeping system and set up books.
8. Project sales and costs of sales.
9. Assess money needs.
10. Incorporate ourselves and assign shares based on invested capital. *Inc. Yourself by* Judith H. McQuown (Harper Business Books) is the definitive book on every aspect of incorporation

and a must read for $25.00. Spend the time and money. They're both well worth it. This book should also be part of our restaurant reference library.

All this to do and we don't even have a signed lease. But we will. I very strongly suggest that at this point we spend time with an experienced restaurant accountant because the right one wants our business and will help us do projections, ledgers, profit and loss work ups and can easily set up all the state and federal accounts at a reasonable rate. Because if we know what we're doing as operators, our accountant will take care of all our accounting needs: payroll, state, federal, corporate, employee and personal.

Business plans usually include projections of fixed expenses and the amount of gross sales needed to cover expenses. It also looks at the competition and projected sales. Whether for ourselves or a formal business plan for investors, the business plan is also the game plan. I've seen many different business plans, but ultimately creating our own business plan is the way to go. It should be specific, brief and not more than three to five pages. Our proposal, which should be double-spaced, neat and professionally packaged, should include the following:

1. Who we are and what we want to borrow funds for.
2. What our qualifications are for opening and running the proposed restaurant concept we've developed.
3. What we believe is special about our concept and the niche our restaurant will be filling.
4. Who and where our customers are and where we'll be located.
5. Our Product's uniqueness compared to nearby competition. Menu, prices, food costs, controlled overhead, hours and how this all works in a market with the great potential of our neighborhood.

6. Our projected first year's operating expenses and our future earnings objectives.
7. How much money we will need.
8. When and how the money will be paid back and at what interest.
9. Our financial histories and what amounts we're investing in the restaurant.
10. Our profit and loss and cash flow by month for the first year and monthly costs of sales.
11. In our summation we have to hammer home why this concept operated and managed by our team is a home run. Remember it's us that people invest in and if we need their money, they need to be sold on our abilities to perform. Also remember that most restaurants fail because they are undercapitalized, so make sure that what we're asking for is more than enough.

Consider this when submitting our business plan to someone: Did they ask for it? Talk is cheap. All the people who know what we're about to do who say they're interested seem to change their tune when our intent becomes serious. Seriously interested people ask for a business plan.

When we give someone our business plan, it is critical that we tell him or her that we need an answer within a specific time frame. If we really need to find funds, time begins to cost money. The day we sign the lease, the clock begins to tick. People who don't get right back to us yet feed us hope are pulling our chain. That's when we move on to the next potential investor.

The most easily understood and helpful books on this subject are:

The Business Planning Guide
Upstart Publishing Company, Inc.
P.O. Box 323, Portsmouth, NH 03801
800-235-8866

A Guide to Preparing a Restaurant Business Plan
from the Business Accounting and Promotion Department of the Library of The National Restaurant Association
800-424-5156, Ext. 5375

Uniform System of Accounts for Restaurants
also from the Business, Accounting and Promotion Department of the Library of the National Restaurant Association.

My N.Y.C. Story Part 3

PULLING OFF A LAZARUS MOVE IN THE RESTAURANT BUSINESS.

How did I get the money to open Fishbones when I didn't have any? I was working nights across the street from the Fishbones site in an old-time, neighborhood Italian restaurant. When I had enough money saved, I ordered the first dumpster. I started emptying Mr. J's club (rather I should say, his shooting gallery) during the day by myself. Of course my heart would skip a beat like it did in East Harlem as I swept up the used needles and crack vials. It took three dumpsters to empty the space, but I knew immediately that the place was too small for what I wanted to do. So I had to pay my new best friend Leon the landlord an extra two hundred dollars a month to lease me the full basement under the space.

    My first month of free rent was ending and friends who had lent me money for the chicken deal were dropping by. Foolishly I told some of them their money was safe and now in my new venture. I'd repay them with interest once I got this effort up and running. Even Mr. Chicken came by and tried to work another deal. Someone I owed money to said: "What are you going to do here?" I replied: "A Californian Mexican restaurant/margarita bar." The next night he brought his father by and the father thought it looked promising but didn't want to put any of his money into it. Did I have a business plan for him to look at? The father also pulled me aside to ask me to pay his son the money I owed him.

So there I was in the empty space of great hopes and dreams feeling like I better get right on this business plan thing. I was going to need to borrow some serious dough, and those who have money hang onto it unless they are presented an opportunity by qualified people that might turn them a good profit on their investment.

But what I felt good about, even though my friend's father wouldn't invest, was that he really liked the location and my rent. So did his son and the son let his chicken money roll into Fishbones (I'll be commenting on this gesture later).

CHAPTER 7

Dealing for the Ideal Deal

7. Dealing for the Ideal Deal

Nothing's written in stone.

Says who? The signing of any real estate deal is a **big deal.** Signing a lease for our restaurant is a major commitment. A bad deal at the beginning has the potential to be legally lethal because landlords, their attorneys and realtors all feed off of you. Applying what we've learned in the earlier chapters can turn this around and landlords can become very cooperative. Real estate people and attorneys can also become very helpful when they get a sense that we know what we want and what we're doing.

Our goal is: *Get the place we've selected at the price that works within our budget, and a landlord who participates in our capitalization of his space.* We want the deal that leaves us comfortable with our rent. It doesn't matter if it's a mortgage payment, rent check or a lease option payment, it's due the first of every month. We definitely don't want a killer rent that makes the landlord a partner.

What we have to pay particular attention to here is the restaurant rent axiom: **Rent cannot exceed 10% of our projected gross.** This is clearly stamped on the back of the Warning Plaque. If the rent is more than our projections can handle, we need a cooperative landlord who will take less at the start of the lease. This isn't a big deal but it can significantly shrink the down side and help us keep on budget.

What all landlords everywhere want is a good tenant with long-term acceptability. How does a landlord get this tenant? The landlord waits until someone with the right track record walks into his office or someone without the right track record, but who knows what he wants and how to go about it. A landlord will participate because failures don't yield rent, only headaches and legal fees.

Landlords that work with us are not adversarial. They understand seasons, storms and the unexpected. They also understand that any tenant they can relate to and give and take with is of great value compared to the clunkers they're used to. Dealing with landlords shouldn't be an intimidating experience but is because almost all of us have never dealt with commercial leasing. Somehow we empower landlords simply because they own the property and have something we want. We'll never know how they got what we want. What we want to know is how can they help us? If they can't, if they don't want to, and if all they are is bad news, walk away.

We should always feel good about leaving situations that don't serve our goal. Our commitment to our project is so complete that it is damn important that this first binding step be structured in such a way that it is no longer a factor in our pre-production. Rather, it is an agreeable and understood fixed expense in our monthly budget.

Any lawyer or realtor can tell you there are a million ways to skin the proverbial cat in real estate deals. Then after having said that they'll fight to sell you the landlord's deal. That's why we've narrowed our choices down to three different sites in the restaurant graveyard.

We have the floor plans and have been at the different locations with our engineer, the building inspector, and the health inspector. We now have a pretty good idea of what it will cost at each site to put on our production. The time we spent with various officials didn't cost us anything but it certainly accomplished a lot. So did having the engineer there even though he was paid.

These people sent a message to the landlord's camp that tells him we're serious and professional. It shows that we've done our homework and know the relative value of the asking rent in the present condition of the space. Now we can negotiate with the realtor, his lawyer, or the landlord directly with the confidence of knowing that one of our three locations is going to work or we'll just keep looking.

What I call the restaurant graveyard is just a segment of the rental market in which realtors, landlords and the former operators of the space have given up on trying to make a buck on the deal. The former operators have walked away and left the space for dead.

Usually the landlord was owed rent and took possession of the space and has auctioned off anything of value. Gone are the fixtures, equipment and the fixture fee. What's often left is a For Rent sign in the window of a stripped down space that looks like it was bombed. But for some reason the space begins to look different to us and keeps us awake at night as the creative process begins. In our waking thoughts we'll continually work on the make over of the space until we've turned it into a theater that can comfortably house our production, within our budget. We now have an advantage at this stage. Here's why:

1. We have a motivated landlord who'll be very interested in talking to us and willing to make some concessions so his unsightly dead space can return to the rent roll.
2. The space was a restaurant before and since we won't be making any structural changes, there are no building permits or building professional services required. And there aren't construction insurance costs to incur.
3. In pre-existing restaurant spaces you'll most always find expensive items left behind that the landlord just couldn't get rid of such as: restrooms or restroom plumbing, kitchen plumbing, grease traps, exhaust hoods and fans, and existing electrical lines.
4. The best thing about the spaces we've selected is that they have characteristics that work with our concept. The places can be broom swept clean and painted out in two weeks with us doing the work.
5. None of the spaces have restrictions or limitations according to homework we've done.

It's time to make an offer.

For our purposes, let's say all three offers we made through realtors to landlords had positive responses. The landlord who owned our first choice had no intention of letting us have the space without his getting up front money for the fixtures. That figure was $10,000 and not negotiable. What he was offering in the lease agreement was:

- A ten-year lease starting at $4,000 a month with a 2.5% increase each year.
- Ninety days free rent during construction.
- A space under 2,000 sq.ft. without storage, but he would give us basement space elsewhere in the building at no added cost. Taxes will be pro-rated only on rented space.
- First, last and security deposit of $12,000 required.

The rest of this landlord's lease could have tied up Houdini: Twenty-nine pages of legal jabber-talk.

We'll take the lease to our real estate attorney because we can't even get this landlord to take or return our calls. The attorney got through to his attorney and was able to get four months free rent and a reduction of the deposits to $8,000. On the surface it looks like we're $18,000 out of pocket before we even get the keys to the place.

Something is amiss. It might have been different if the equipment he wanted the fixture fee to cover was of some use to us, but it wasn't. It was old junk and nothing we could use.

"So what do you want to do," asked the attorney? We said, "Let's meet with this landlord and see what we can do."

The meeting you, our attorney and I went to was a two hundred and fifty dollar mistake. His fee was a waste of money because the landlord was a nasty dirt ball. He made Mr. Potter in "Its a Wonderful Life" look like Mother Theresa. Everything we tried to do to make him see it our way was met with a caustic remark.

I'll go as far as most in being civil but if someone crosses the line I'll tell 'em so. After he said something stupid to our lawyer I turned to him and asked him calmly, "Did you just take your shoes off? Something stinks here and I don't like that or your stinkin' thinkin'." I said a few more things to his lackey attorney and we left.

On the train ride home we decided on another of the sites. We met with a completely different type of landlord and made a deal we're all happy with. The figures are outlined in the next chapter.

My N.Y.C. Story Part 4

PLAYING "LET'S MAKE A DEAL" AT FISHBONES

I was well into my second dumpster when a guy who had dated a friend of mine stopped by and we started talking.

He was from Southern California and knew a little about that lifestyle, but nothing about Mexican food or running a restaurant. However, between this guy and his friend, they had fifty grand and no plans.

His friend arrived and he and I hit it off immediately. We'll call him Dylan. We were almost the same age and had a mutual respect for what each other could do. He was a builder with vast restaurant construction experience and a tremendous work ethic. I was the creative one that could convince him this whole concept of a fun Southern Californian Lifestyle Mexican Rocking Bar idea could work on Columbus Avenue in New York City. I also brought the same work ethic and acquired restaurant experience to our effort.

Unfortunately, Dylan's friend was very different, whether purposefully or by nature. It was clear that he was neither in my sensibility loop nor in Dylan's. We'll call him Fred. Fred's work ethic was different from ours and his restaurant background was zip. But in my burning desire to get the project done, I put up with Fred and his inane behavior. I planned on taking care of him later.

Dylan and I worked on a business plan that showed we needed an estimated additional $60,000 to complete the project. All those people that I knew who were so interested were suddenly missing. And some others that we gave the plan to just jerked us around or asked for outlandish concessions.

My investment was valued at $25,000. The buddies' investment was the $50,000 cash, which was dwindling away as we worked on and on. There we were, in the middle of a classic restaurant mistake: Running out of money with very little serious interest from any money sources we knew.

We even got to the point where we were working long hours and drawing no pay, which was nothing to begin with. Dylan did the bookkeeping, Fred complained a lot, and I worked and worried while the interior started to take shape.

One summer weekend my girlfriend had gone to visit her parents in Idaho and the guys went to Long Island to party. I stayed in the city and did a lot of drywall work on the place. It got very warm, so I left the front doors open and met a lot of people who lived in the neighborhood. They couldn't wait until our place was opened. Of course, that furthered my resolve. I was determined to find the money somewhere.

One of the faces that popped in that weekend was a doctor who called me and made an offer: He would put up the needed funding, but he wanted a 35% equity position and two points above prime on his loan, which was to be paid out first.

Now, *think about* that offer. What would you do?

I called a friend of mine and ran the offer by him for his expert feedback. He had me talk to his businessman father about our situation and the doctor's offer. My friend's father, who we'll call Mr. X, very succinctly instructed me on how he would structure the deal.

First, I was the producer with the lease and the idea driving the project, so my position was greater in equity value than any one else who was participating. If I felt they could deliver and perform in other capacities after opening, the two partners' position should be valued at no more than 39%. He said he liked what he was hearing and if I wanted him to, he would drop in on us next week when he came to visit his daughter who was attending Bard College in Upstate New York.

Before we finished I asked him about the remaining 61% in the deal and what was his suggestion to counter the doctor's offer? He laughed and told me to forget about the doctor. If he was happy with what he saw when he visited the site he'd put up the money we needed to finish the project at the same interest plus a 25% stake in the total.

His last words were: "Now how's your math, Bill?"

I answered: "36% better, I think."

CHAPTER 8

Our Budget

8. Our Budget

Never underestimate the amount of money you will need and what it will cost you to open a restaurant. I know that's a big, ugly statement, but as we progress through these chapters, I hope the line through all of this is becoming apparent. That line is: If we don't have all our ducks in a row, our lives are going to be a lot different than the Marx Brothers lives in "Duck Soup."

We've gone from the desire to own our own restaurant to the *why* of wanting that dream to be realized. We've learned about the mandatory skills and experience needed to manage that dream and desire. We know where, how and why we want to do it. We've done the business plan and have tried to be realistic and accurate in our projections. And now we have to do the hardest part: Ask for the right amount of money.

Even in our modestly proposed Mom and Pop fifty-to-sixty seater we better have or have access to *twice* the projected costs or we should forget it. And we should never borrow or risk more than we can afford to lose. Remember that investors want personal guarantees on their loans. So if your efforts fail, they've got their loaned money back with accrued interest.

Let that sink in for a moment. The lost money when paid back, plus interest, could, in time, be more than the original loan. Broadway producers have ways of structuring their investment plans so that if they and their investors go down it's a write off and they'll try to make it right on the next deal. Believe me, restaurant investors don't walk away so easily. Neither do the purveyors. And bankruptcy doesn't make sense to relatives, friends or loved ones. They all want their money back quickly and with interest.

My parallel story about Fishbones illustrates that hard work, a great idea and location can't overcome the high price of borrowing money from an opportunistic businessman's deal. Any makeover of a restaurant space into a hipster-dipster eatery in New York City is easily a $250,000 investment. The recent make over of Fishbones is in excess of $300,000 and it had to open before it was completed to try and slow down the $15,000 a month rent meter. Egos fuel these expenses because common sense seems to give way to the visions, schemes and themes of people who advise these egos that their idea was great, but by making some changes it can be greater. Hence, here's my bill. That's the cutting edge hustle of New York City and without a doubt it can produce places that take our breath away or debt that takes years to retire.

The money for these restaurants comes from a variety of investor sources. Most are partnerships, either Limited or General (the number of investors distinguishes the difference between the two). There are also working partnerships and silent or sleeping partners. Working partnerships are the only feasible possibility. A silent partnership is like jumbo shrimp or military intelligence—it's an oxymoron.

Any and all investors bring their opinionated friends and families to a venture and drive you nuts. When they see some business being done they want to look at the books and ask questions about legitimate expenses. I've already said it enough: People with money only let go of it to get a better grip on it! It's better to save and wait until you have enough money of your own to open a restaurant, because you'll damn sure know what you want and how to do it without any one looking over your shoulder questioning your expenses.

Can you imagine bringing these different investors to the sites that interested us? No way!

Can you imagine them being involved in the look of our place? Not!

Could you imagine them being involved in the menu, the menu pricing or our Northern Italian cuisine concept? Never ever, ever!

Clearly we must have enough saved to start our own business or be willing to give up our sanity.

Working partnerships, like all relationships, are not easy. It's best to have a history with each other beforehand. Also, it's best for each partner to bring capital to the venture. If the funds are not equal and the responsibilities are, legal expertise can help design a partnership contract that makes a better but equal marriage between the prospective partners. The funds are the budget and it's best to have all money details taken care of before you go any further than the signing of a lease.

As working partners, our original concept budgeted our restaurant at $100,000. We've signed the lease using our DBA name, Tusculum, and have incorporated and worked out partnership details. Also, at our lawyer's urging, each partner signed a one page Buy/Sell agreement. This one page document is the way out for either partner if the relationship sours. It's a smart precaution.

In our partnership the split is 50-50 down the middle. Each of us has $50,000 cash, the necessary experiences to handle our different responsibilities and a mutual respect for each other's work ethic. Paolo (you) will run the back of the house and I'll run the front. At the end of each business night, we'll reconcile our receipts together and discuss what's needed for tomorrow. That's how we'll operate and communicate what each of us needs done.

The time we spend together is crucial. It keeps us focused and in sync. So let's sit down soon to do the budget. We're signing the lease tomorrow!

Sometimes everything works out for the best. The space that was our second choice had more useable space, equipment and a motivated landlord. The landlord grew up in the brownstone that housed the empty restaurant space. Our concept really appealed to him and he conceded that the space originally was his parent's Irish family-style restaurant. His parents ran that restaurant for thirty years and retired and returned to Ireland after putting five children through college and buying the building.

The landlord was a very articulate college teacher who loved his neighborhood and knew it intimately. We could see he was excited about our concept, our experience and desire. He was also fair minded and annually visited Italy with his family and they loved Tuscan foods. He thought the neighborhood would thoroughly enjoy and support our efforts. When push came to shove and we asked him about reducing his asking rent, he said in one long sentence. "My wife and I will be away this summer and when we return we will want a table for twenty friends and family if you agree to treat us that night. That will be your first month's rent. Until then the place is yours to begin with rent free."

This all happened two days before Easter. The agreed lease was for ten years starting at $3200 a month. He waved any up front money until the end of the year so we could use that money to do other things. At year's end we will owe him the first and last month's rent. The annual rent increase is two percent. The fixtures, equipment and everything left in the space are ours to use.

He told us to have our lawyer visit him and he would work out the details with him.

After shaking hands on the deal we left and floated down the street more excited than when the Rangers won the Cup. We've got a shot at winning the title: "*I know this great little Italian place.*" We've got almost five months free rent. We could be open in two months and spend the summer off-season time perfecting our production for a fall opening.

And now, to our budget.

Our General Budget for Tusculum, $100,000

Department (Responsibility)	Projected $

Legal (Both of ours)
  Incorporation of Tusculum
  Lease consultation and negotiations
  Liquor License filing
  Balance = $95,000
	5,000

Site Lease (Both of ours)
    First and Last months rent set aside   6,400
    Balance = $88,600

Improvements until opening (Both of ours)
    Kitchen equipment upgrade and repairs   8,500
    Bar and bathroom repairs and upgrades   3,500
    Store front door and new lettered awning   4,000
    Paint, plaster, wallpaper, mirrors, wall   4,000
        sconces for lighting effects, wall-mounted
        vases for flowers
    Subtotal = $20,000
    Balance = $68,600

Accounting (Both of Ours)   4,000
    Set up Federal I.D. #
    Set up State I.D. # and sales tax account #
    Set up payroll account
    Consultation and Advice
    Balance = $64,600

    Our General Budget for Tusculum, $100,000 (Cont'd)
Department (Responsibility)   **Projected $**

Permits (Both of ours)
    Permits required for our makeover—NONE
    Licenses required to operate:
        -Health Department Permit   500
        -Wine and Beer License   2,000
    Balance = $62,100

Insurance (Both of ours)   8,000
    Includes wrap around Liability—Fire,
        Liquor, and Burglary plus: Glass breakage
        Content damage, Business interruption,
        State Disability, Worker's Compensation.
        Landlord named as an additional insured.
        Payment to the insurance company
        is $2000 every ninety days.
    Balance = $54,100

Kitchen Startup Expenses (Paolo's)   11,000
    Includes food inventory for opening,
        kitchen utensils and china for 60.
    Balance = $43,100

Bar Startup Expenses (Mine)
    Wine, beer and water for opening   3,500
    Restaurant glassware: 200, 10oz. wine   600
        glasses used for wine, water and beer.
    Electronic cash register with different   800
        compartments to breakdown sales
    Ice machine, soda system, and espresso   1,100
        are rented from one company requiring a
        $750 deposit and $350 for soda and gas tanks.
    Balance = $37,100

Our General Budget for Tusculum, $100,000 (Cont'd)
Department (Responsibility)	Projected $
Dining and Bar Area Furnishing (Mine)	2,000

Repairing existing bar and dining room furniture, plus the cost of materials for reupholstering chairs and tables.
Balance = $35,100

Office Expenses (Both of ours)	3,000

File cabinets, desk, chairs, computer, printer and office supplies.
Balance = $32,100

Additional Expenses (Both of ours)	2,100

Utility deposits and out-of-pocket expenses for whatever is needed.
Balance = $30,000

TOTAL START-UP EXPENSES	70,000

Balance = $30,000

And you thought it couldn't be done, but we've accomplished it here and it's done all around the world by people who do their homework and watch every dollar. The key to the deal was the Lease, no question about that. As you gain experience in how deals are made you'll be able to create win-win situations that benefit both parties.

Our cooperating landlord and all the useable equipment at the restaurant site saved us a lot of money.

Our hard work in doing almost everything ourselves saved us a lot of money also. By paying everyone up front and putting our first and last months' rent aside, we have a realistic balance that will see us through the better part of our first year. If we don't use it, it's still a good feeling to know we've got some backup capital. But the glue that sealed the deal absolutely, aside from the lease, was our knowing what we wanted and how to clearly go about it, and our negotiation of a favorable result with a landlord who recognized the potential of our concept. You might think he gave us a lot, but actually it will all come back quite profitably to him over the years. This is a great way to begin with it all feeling so right.

My N.Y.C. Story Part 5

MR. X VISITS THE FISHBONES SITE

On a beautiful and bright sunny afternoon when everyone was outdoors, Mr. X came to the site and gave it a walk-through. We handed him our business plan and proposal for the completion of the project, and we answered his questions. Dylan was able to handle most of the construction details and I talked about the concept, menu, type of bar and the running of the restaurant. When I was done I brought us all out into the warm sunshine and showed Mr. X our customers. The street was full of traffic and the sidewalks filled with the neighborhood residents returning from work. The people would run into their apartments, change their clothes and head for Central Park (or wherever), but they were out in force and Mr. X did not miss that.

Mr. X shook hands with the guys, chatted for a while and then told them he wanted to speak to me privately.

They went back to work and we went across the street to the restaurant where I worked at night. My boss had Bass Ale on tap and we had a few. I introduced Mr. X to my boss and within five minutes they were talking about business and how much they each liked my idea and location.

He was sold on the whole idea. The only thing he didn't like was Fred. In his eyes, the guy was a loser. Mr. X didn't sugarcoat his opinions. But I felt an obligatory connection because Fred and his money brought Dylan and into the deal. I needed Dylan to get it done and Dylan had contributed a lot to the deal. Mr. X really liked the expertise and experience Dylan brought to the project, so I guess Mr. X could live with two out of three because he told me: "Count me in. My lawyer's here doing some work with my son and me. Why don't you tell those guys the deal I mentioned to you last week and we can sign some papers and get the place opened? I think it's a super location and if Fred becomes a problem we'll get rid of him!"

At this stage we had only talked to a Liquor License Attorney and I called him up and explained our good fortune with Mr. X. He agreed to represent us at the next meeting because he could also get all the Liquor License application papers signed so they could be submitted. The guys had no problem with Mr. X's offer and so we eagerly went to the meeting at the site that evening.

Mr. X's attorney gave our lawyer a five-page document. Columbo took his time reading and said he wanted to speak to us alone.

We said, "Sure." What did we know? We thought we'd sign the papers, get the money, finish the project and have a partner in Idaho.

Well, Columbo told us what was up with that five-page document. For lending us $75,000 at 2% above Prime we were giving Mr. X 25% of our stock and signing personal guarantees. Not only that, if the restaurant failed, Mr. X took possession of all assets including the lease—and we would still owe him the principle. Mr. X's final statement said there was no deal if he couldn't put into place accountants who he approved. Then Columbo added: "Gentlemen. I don't know this guy or care how you know him, but this is suicide. Christ, you better look and see if he has a shark fin sticking out of his suit! This is a 'no-way-out-deal' for you guys. And another thing, that backdoor of the school across the street better move or disappear because this place has been in violation of Liquor Authority rules for years. There isn't a grandfather clause that carries over. The school takes precedence."

You cannot imagine how I felt after those comments. I told Columbo: "That 'no-way-out-deal' is the only shot we've got! If we have to pay to play, then so be it. And, I've walked off those 200 feet from our front door and the school's backdoor several times. It's exactly 207 feet."

They said nothing. What could they say? Their money was gone. They had worked hard and believed in what they were doing. Losing some points wasn't going to be a deal killer in a suicide deal.

Columbo then asked if we understood what we were doing. We all nodded yes and had no clue. We signed the papers and shook on the deal. I didn't sleep that night because after everyone left I kept re-measuring the distance between our door and the school's door. It always came up short.

When I walked off the distance, I got 200 feet. But when I measured it with a tape, I was eight feet short. The Liquor guy would measure with a tape, so now we were going to have to move the front door and that was a major project.

For sure, we were hog-tied by the deal, but that didn't deter my desire to get the place open. I didn't feel vulnerable. I felt lucky.

I worked harder and started feeling that my relationship with Dylan was closer than the one with Mr. X. I started confronting Fred on all his stupid stuff. He worked better and sometimes he listened.

To my credit, I bought some basic business books and learned how to read different business reports and statements. Through Columbo we found some mutually acceptable accountants for Mr. X.

Summer faded away and fall changed the leaves in the park and our neighborhood. On the day we were going to move the front door over 10 feet, I made one more measurement. I still came up short.

There was a lot of activity at the school that day and a friendly face with a French accent introduced himself to me and wondered what I was doing. He was the school's principal. They were receiving Haitian children from all over the city in a new program that started this week.

He was a good guy doing good work and I trusted him, so I told him exactly the pickle I was in. In exchange, he told me the pickle he was in and that any appropriate contribution to the school's computer needs would be appreciated. It would be appreciated so much, in fact, that if I knew when the Liquor Authority official would be taking his measurements, he would, in kind, conduct a fire drill out the school's back door and direct the guy to the school's front door.

We made the contribution and every day I watched and waited for the Liquor Authority guy. When he showed up, I called the principal. Then I distracted the guy with my tape measure while the school ran a fire drill. The kids filled the corner of the block and the principal directed the Liquor Authority guy, tape measure in hand, to the front door of the school.

That's the day I learned that sometimes you make your own luck.

CHAPTER 9

Our Concept

9. Our Concept

A well-executed, original idea in the restaurant business when done with attention to detail, no matter how simple, can have startling results. It's amazing what the ever-wary customer's critical eyes pick out. But, when that customer feels comfortable in a restaurant space, his or her word-of-mouth, two-word review can start the ball rolling with: "Great place!"

We all listen to what friends say about movies, plays or new restaurants because we are always looking to reward ourselves with experiences that are pleasing. When people bad-mouth a restaurant, they usually have legitimate reasons. And even though the problems may have been corrected, those people don't stop talking down the place. Does the restaurant suffer? To some extent, certainly it does. The more problems a restaurant has, the more disgruntled former customers you have spreading bad reviews.

Nailing down your concept and making some smart choices in execution can eliminate many problems right from the beginning. In the same way we've wound up where we are with our restaurant business plan, location selection, lease signing and budget planning, we have to continue to **work at it**. Work is the art of the deal. Once again we're going to put down on paper what we want to accomplish and how we're going to do it.

Our leased site has a twenty-four foot wide storefront and is sixty-five feet deep with full basement. The access to the basement is through a sidewalk delivery entrance and a staircase in the kitchen. This means our street level space is a 1560 square foot box with a useable basement.

So let's draw that box. Not from the realtor's floor plan, but off our critical measurements, which must include the details of the existing layout. Where, exactly, does the dining room begin and end? Where is the bar and the plumbing for the bar? Measure the exact locations of the restrooms and the specific dimensions of the kitchen. We should diagram the existing kitchen equipment, especially plumbing and electrical sources, in detail.

Now, draw an outline of the box space and make several copies of it, because we are going to spend a lot of time laying out the space so that it effectively and efficiently serves our concept. The ideas that have existed in our minds and all our conversations must now transcend the imagined to the nuts and bolts of doing it within our budget. So let's get the space cleaned out and get rid of everything we'll never use. Once this is done, we can better walk through the space, address our different needs and come up with possible solutions on paper.

When we first decided on our Northern Italian Restaurant, our idea was very simple. We wanted only fifty to sixty seats, an exposed kitchen, a staff of six, five hours a night, six nights a week to serve a hearty, robust menu and time to enjoy our lives. That was our idea and that became our concept. We've made many decisions based on that concept. So even though it now looks like we could have a larger restaurant in our cleaned out space, we're sticking to our original plan. Small, tight and right is all we need for our opening. If we see an overwhelming demand for our product, we'll consider other choices in the future.

I'm big on the visual aspect of a restaurant. My influence goes way back to a place in San Francisco that my parents would take everyone to on special occasions. It was a Mom and Pop restaurant with forty or fifty seats, a small bar, and a three-item menu. Oh yes, and off to the side of the bar was one of those machines that if the old man was in the mood, he gave us dimes to play. The dime gave the operator two minutes to grab with claws for untold riches. Of course, it also gave me time to steal the cherries out of my sisters' Shirley Temples while they were the operators.

In time, we were seated and on lucky nights we got to sit in a booth with curtains. My parents probably liked that booth before the five of us were born, but now anytime we made the booth into a fort, we were told: "One more God-damn word out of any of you and you're all going to the parking lot!"

My father might be tried for war crimes in today's restaurant world, but back then he had kids that knew how to behave in restaurants.

Anyway, there were a lot of warm sour dough bread and butter on the table. Homemade minestrone soup would always arrive immediately after you sat down.

I can't remember the lady's name that took our order, but by some act of God she remembered ours all the time, for all those years. "Chicken, steak or crabs, all served with salad and pasta," she'd say. We were crab lovers and some how my parents knew how to order enough so there was nothing left over. And if you fell asleep, you missed out on the homemade cannolis.

Now, if you believe that a restaurant's menu defines the concept, the aforementioned concept could not be more simple and efficient. A three-item menu with soup, salad, pasta and dessert is a thing of beauty and to this day still packs them in. Although the restaurant is four times larger, the decor and menu remain the same. It's still a Mom and Pop operation, but after nearly a hundred years, it's a landmark. I'll bet the current owners wouldn't change a single thing about the place for love or money.

I believe the menu is the most important part of the concept. The menu dictates the design of the kitchen and requires certain kitchen personnel. It also has inventory requirements and controls. The food cost of menu items affects our prices and must be designed to attract our customers.

Visual presentation, otherwise known as "atmosphere" is the other important element in our concept. What's the place going to look like and feel like? Casual dining is definitely what we're after and that will be reflected in the comfortable design of the space we're now cleaning out.

Remember the restaurant I mentioned early on where I went with my wife's parents on her birthday (to jog your memory, they paid the bill)? I want to take you back there because that was an interesting and wonderfully executed concept. The restaurant was new and built from the ground up with no expense spared. To me, the concept was simply a large Mom and Pop dining room in a cozy farmhouse. At the back of the room was an exposed, state-of-the-art kitchen joined on one side with an in-house bakery and a forty-foot bar on the other side of the room.

Where's the Mom and Pop in this place? It started with a successful Italian restaurateur who decided to build a restaurant for his sister that reminded them of their grandfather's house and the wonderful meals their grandfather made.

To be sure, their new restaurant was larger than grandfather's house, but the design of the dining room was simple, homey and cozy. The menu and wine lists were both straightforward and offered affordable quality.

After the personable waiter took our drink order, a young woman came to the table with a bottle of olive oil and a warm loaf of terrific bread called striatta. She poured oil on our bread plates and passed around the bread. I love eating bread that way and by the time our waiter returned with our drinks and took our dinner orders the bread was gone and more arrived.

We each had an appetizer. I selected a $12 bottle of wine that I knew was no longer available in my friend's liquor store, but when it was we drank it. 1992 Cabernets never disappoint, but as my friend Carol says: "1991 Californian Cabernets are superb, sublime wines to die for, darling!" This wine was more expensive in her store when they could get it than it was here. Little by little I've learned a lot about fine wines from Carol and her husband Bob and this wine list showed me that this operator knew his way around the wine industry. To serve these wines at these prices you have to buy in volume. Our first taste after the birthday toast made us all glad that he bought in volume. The price was great value and the taste was just what Carol said it would be. Thankfully, she's helping to compose Tusculum's wine list.

Dinner came and everything was terrific. I had been silently watching the owner's sister supervise the dining room staff. The woman wasn't very outgoing and she didn't interact much with customers, but her staff did. I thought to myself, "Not my style," but the results were excellent.

The birthday desserts were over-the-top and while the family was drinking their coffees, I got up and went on a tour of the restaurant—that's when my father-in-law paid the check that was supposed to be mine. I talked to the chef and he took me through the bakery and prep room. He let me get behind the exposed kitchen's line. I was very impressed with his setup. He told me he had had no input into the kitchen's design, but appreciated it nonetheless. "It's built for seasonal speed, Man," he said.

"I'll bet that kitchen is going to be very busy in the summer and fall," I told my wife back at the table while I was waiting for the check that never came. The operational part of the restaurant was high-tech, but the overall feeling was personable and familiar. It was a nice night and the feeling I left with reminded me of those Mom and Pop experiences from my past.

The underlined text sums up so well what this restaurant succeeded in doing for our party and many other customers. All the different elements of our dining experience added up to making us all *feel good*. To me that is the Product we want to sell in our restaurant.

We stopped by that Italian restaurant the next day to pick up some of that bread we had had the night before from the retail bakery outlet in the back of the restaurant. It's strange what good bread can make people do. Just because good bread and butter or olive oil are giveaways, most restaurants try to cut corners on the expense, but that's not what we're going to do!

The two examples of the old and new Mom and Pop operations I've used hopefully shed some light on how to incorporate our concept and ideas into how we might lay out our kitchen and dining room.

Paolo has worked up a hearty Tuscan menu that we're excited about and I've come up with a dining room and kitchen design that works for us; so let's see how it looks on paper.

Paolo's Menu

When customers are seated, warm garlic bread is put on their table with glasses of ice, lemon slices and bottled water. They are then asked for their drink orders and given menus. The drinks are served and questions regarding menu details are answered.

ANTIPASTI
Firenze: Parmesan slices, prosciutto, roasted red peppers, olives, mozzarella and marinated Portobello mushrooms.
Siena: Smoked mozzarella on roasted red peppers, red onion and tomatoes dressed in oil and herb vinegar.

ACQUACOTTA
Zuppa Di Fagioli: White bean soup with ham.
Infarninata: Minestrone with Polenta.

INSALATAS
Fried Calamari, fried eggplant, fried zucchini mixed with white beans and shallots. Light lemon and olive oil dressing.
A Spinach Caesar with grilled chicken slices.

PASTAS

Rigatoni alla Buttera: Peasant-style penne pasta with sweet and spicy sausages.

Spaghetti alla Fornaia e Funghi: Baker's Spaghetti with Porcini mushrooms and walnut sauce.

Lasagne con Spinach e Funghi: Vegetarian lasagna.

Linguine con Gli Scampi: Linguine with Shrimp in a Shrimp sauce.

VEGETARIAN PLATTER

Gurguglione e Funghi Gratella: Sautéed zucchini, peppers, tomatoes, green beans and small roasted potatoes mixed with grilled Porcini and Shiitake mushrooms.

MEAT AND FISH

Pollo Al Vino Russo: Braised chicken in Red Wine sauce with baby onions and mushrooms served over thin slices of Polenta.

Pollo alla Cacciatora: Hunter's styled chicken stewed with garlic, rosemary, thyme, sage, onions, tomatoes and enough wine. Served over wild rice.

Polpettone alla Aretina: Meatloaf from Arezza, stuffed with mushrooms and served with orange apricot sauce.

Ossobuco Al Vino e Tarragone: Veal shank in wine and Tarragon sauce with Arborio rice and topped with Gremolata.

Costata alla Florentina: Florentine marinated T-Bone Steaks, grilled and covered with olive oil, herbs and Porcini mushrooms.

Pesce all' Olio di Oliva ed Erbe Fresche: Baked Catch-of-the-Day in olive oil lemon herb sauce.

DESSERT
   Coffee on a fork—Baked coffee-flavored pudding served warm with whipped cream and eaten with a fork.
   All coffees served with Munchy Bones, lemon-almond wafers.

This eleven-item menu is simple, hearty, robust and diverse. It also clearly informs the reader that they will be eating homemade Tuscan specialties from the kitchens of hunters, peasants, and the great family cooks of Tuscany.

Paolo figured our food costs at about 30-34% of our projected sales volume. Based on our projected sales, our intuitive restaurant knowledge and the Prime Cost Method, we can now price out our menu items. The Prime Cost Method uses the food cost of the menu item and the target food cost percentage for the restaurant. In our case, we'll take our menu item #10 (Costata alla Florentina) food cost, which is $5.80 and divide it by our highest targeted food cost percentage. This translates roughly to a menu price of $15.95 for our 10-ounce T-bone steak plate.

Menu pricing is an important restaurant management skill. If we were to mess up this part of the program our potential profitability would be gone and so would we.

Setting it up correctly in the beginning saves a lot of trouble down the road in this business. For example, unused space in our rented site costs us money and yields no income.

Rented space, no matter the location, is the bane of a restaurateur's existence. Why? Because we all tirelessly struggle to serve our customers and make a buck, but so many variables can factor into the income of our business, like weather, holidays and televised sports playoffs. Remember, landlords never skip a beat. So in reality, if we're renting and not buying, "there ain't nuttin' goin' on but the rent every day!" That's why Paolo and I worked a lot of hours on trying to maximize the dining area of the space we've rented. Our projected sales are based on the amount of seats in our dining room for two seatings a night and two to three seatings on Friday and Saturday night. We conservatively guess what each seat will eat and drink and come up with an average check total per customer that we can use to compile our projected sales gross. When we back out the operating costs and various expenses from our projected gross, the numbers will tell us if we're sitting in the sweet spot or the back seat.

If you're working for ten cents profit on every dollar, you're mired in huge numbers and need volume to support your enterprise. But in our Mom and Pop way of doing business, our food, liquor, fixed and labor cost run around 65-70% of our projected sales because we're the owners and operators. Management costs and benefits don't factor into our business and eat up 10 to 15%. In the Mom and Pop restaurant business, it's not what you make but what you take! If your numbers are in what's called the Gold Zone, you're on your way and should proceed.

Our menu also invokes a response that feels like the dining room should be warm with rich colors. Light terra-cotta walls with hunter green trim and a sand-colored ceiling with large ceiling fans. The lighting is from wall sconces that I'll make. They'll be cutouts of chickens, rabbits, fish, sunflowers, stars and moons. Around the three restaurant walls are the sconces with wall vases in between, holding fresh seasonal flowers.

Now let's look at how function follows form in the makeover designs we created for the dining area and kitchen. As I mentioned earlier, we should make our own detailed drawing of the leased space. In the first drawing, I've purposefully left out some very important details. Can you find them? When we know what we have in the leased space, we're less likely to get jerked around by various people trying to sell us goods or services. To pull operating costs in line we need to have the knowledge of how our little power plant works, so when problems arise, we can quickly handle them.

The omitted details are the most important area we need hands on experience with. They are:

1. The electrical power panel.
2. The plumbing lines to the main drain.
3. The grease trap.
4. The source of heating and air conditioning.
5. The first-aid station.

If we're lucky enough to have friends or relatives in different trades, we can minimize the expense of upgrading the electrical panel and oversizing the main drain to the sewer line. We can also eliminate a big chunk of utility waste by updating the HVAC system (heating, venting and air conditioning). The grease trap that exists is oversize, but filled with stinky waste that's been sitting there for years. We need a service company to clean the hoods and grease traps. God forbid you need it, but the first-aid station in the kitchen should be first class and well stocked.

Because we pay for everything coming and going out of our space we should have an understanding of what electricity, water, sewage, heat and air conditioning, gas and waste removal costs us every day. All these factors weigh into the pricing of our menu (believe it or not). It's better to have fixed the leaking faucets, running toilets, clogged and leaking pipes, faulty wiring and an undersized breaker panel now than later.

'As Is' Leased Space:

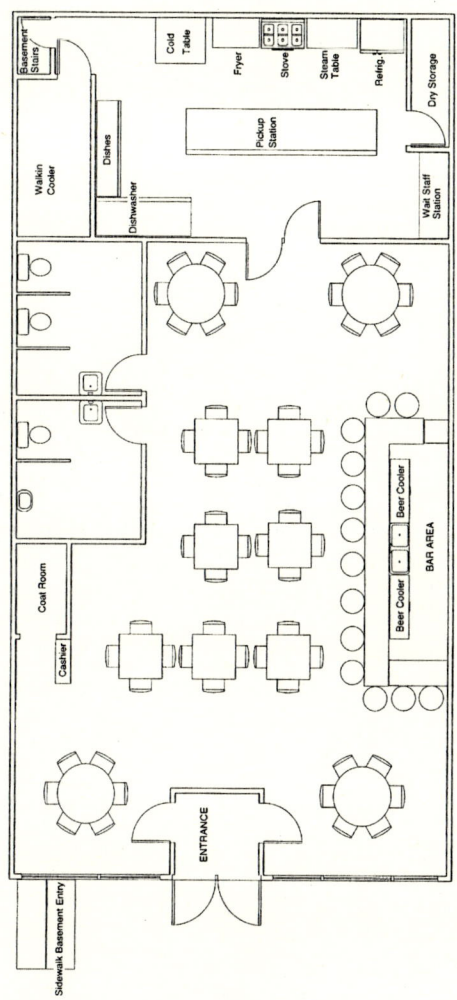

'As Is' Leased Space:

The As Is Leased Space on the previous page is 2,000 square feet including a full basement. Although it's not a bad layout, it has some clumsy and outdated and wasted space. Other features include:

- A half wall of glass across the front.
- A twelve-foot Ansel Fire Hood System over the stove area.
- Seating for approximately 50 to 60 people at tables and twelve or so at the bar.

Modified Leased Space

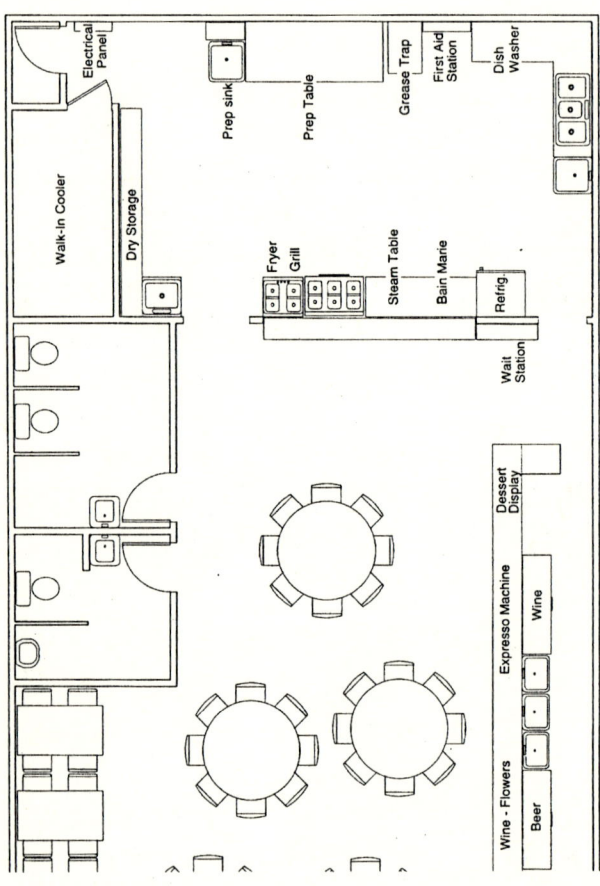

Modified Leased Space

Changes we made to the leased space include:

- The entrance was moved to open up the dining room.
- The cashier station and coatroom were removed. The bar holds the cash register and coat rack, and the hostess stand is at the entrance. We removed the bar stools. This makes the bar the 'control center,' where people are greeted, seated, cashed out and thanked.
- The restrooms were made smaller.
- The dining room has 15 tables that can comfortably seat 80 people.
- The kitchen has been rearranged and is now on display for all customers to see. The wait staff picks up food instantly and returns dirty dishes to the kitchen dirty sink.

The room in the restaurant and kitchen is very accessible and has a nice flow.

Energy is expensive and that expense comes out of our bottom line before we pay ourselves. It costs about a hundred dollars an hour to keep a 50 to 60-seat restaurant like ours powered up and staffed. It adds up so quickly that every consideration we give to effectively managing these expenses over a year's time can save a great deal of money.

With that in mind we, accordingly, laid out our kitchen to serve our re-designed dining room. Our desire to expose the kitchen and to execute our menu means that the hood needs to be moved, as well as all of the re-conditioned kitchen equipment. To keep the heat and odors out of the dining room, we have to increase the size of exhaust hood fan and bring makeup air into the kitchen. That is not in our budget, but very necessary.

Also, we have to oversize the gas line from the main to the kitchen. Again, this is not in our budget, but very necessary. We then thought that the window into the kitchen was also the "pick-up your order counter" and that we need a pass through station to the dishwasher for dirty dishes. We also need a passage way for staff to enter and exit the kitchen safely.

What now emerges when you look at the overview of the floor plan is an oval track. The orders would be picked up on the left side of the pick-up window and served from the left side of the dining room. All the dirty plates would be picked up from the right side of the room and returned to the right side of the kitchen and passed through window. The dining room has a nice flow for wait staff traffic, which makes a very taxing job a little easier.

Everything Paolo needs or wants in his kitchen is at his fingertips. The small space is efficiently laid out around his workstation, which is the eight burner double oven stove. His grill and salamander broiler are at his right hand above the steam table and his vegetables meats, fish and chicken supplies are in the bain-marie. All salads and dressings are in the refrigerator to his left. Anything he needs can be reached for him by the dishwasher/prep man. If he needs to do anything himself, a prep table with a sink is directly behind him.

All of the kitchen design followed the form of our menu, as did the changes in the dining room. What was workable years ago in our leased space no longer serves its purpose. Our new design clearly conveys the sharper, more efficient workability of our concept. When we took the time to put our ideas on paper, different elements appeared as we did the work. The dining room and kitchen evolved into functioning entities following form with attention to detail. Now that's a thing of beauty!

With this task done we now have to re-evaluate our personnel needs. For example, those three round tops can accommodate eight people each. If what we believe and feel is going to happen from day one, we better be prepared. Bad service can ruin everything and the money saved by having a small crew during opening week can never offset the damage done by bad or painfully slow service.

Paolo is going to have three guys plus himself and I'm going to have four wait staff, one bus person, a hostess and myself. Our 50 to 60-seat restaurant can easily be 80 to 90 seats, so we better adjust our staff needs to be as prepared as possible for a great beginning.

Service is, by far, more important than the food or drink put on the table—just ask any three-star restaurant owner. They'll confirm the fact that *service is everything.*

My N.Y.C. Story Part 6

FORTUNE (MOSTLY) SMILES

I knew Fishbones was going to do some serious business the day I found the letters for the front of the store. The eighteen-inch stainless steel letters were to go above the front window, which was trimmed in stainless steel. We restored the storefront and installed black glass. It was sharp looking.

The Zingone Brothers sold us their old "7 Up" awning and we put it on our storefront. I wrote out *Fishbones* in my script and drew a swordfish outline around the letters. Our logo came alive and clearly made a Californian statement that was very different from the New York City norm. That simple logo told you, "This is a fun place serving up good food and great Margaritas." Eddie, the local sign painter, came and painted our name in bright colors and large script on the front window. The whole storefront looked very cool when he was through.

To this day I'll never understand why people cover up storefronts and do all the inside work first. The last thing they do is the storefront. A lot of people passed Fishbones for months and became good customers before we even opened because they loved the way it looked and because I would take the time to talk about it with them and answer their questions.

The day the awning repair guy came to tune up the awning, I came up with: *Fishbones Bar and Restaurant with other stores in Japan, Australia, Vietnam, Brazil and Mars.* With that on the awning flaps, a New York Times reporter stuck her head in the door and asked for an explanation—which I gave her. Two weeks later our concept was in the New York Times and the phone started ringing.

It was late fall when we finally passed our liquor license requirements and were issued a license. We built the kitchen and I started looking for a cook. I knew exactly the type of menu I wanted. It was California/Mexican all the way. Somebody introduced us to a nice young Mexican man from L.A. who was a struggling actor in New York and looking for work. His acting abilities were greater than his cooking abilities. But through him we met a young Salvadorian named Jorge who could cook exactly what I wanted, the way I wanted.

The actor, Jorge and I worked through the creation of our menu and I was very pleased when Jorge and some of his friends said they would come to work for us. I then planned the actor's exit from the kitchen right after we opened.

Through my own personal experience, I knew who the best bartender on the Upper West Side was and I took Dylan to watch him. When Steven was working behind a packed bar he was a human octopus. He didn't tolerate nonsense and because of that he had a legion of beautiful women friends and customers. His passion was ballet, until he blew up his knee, but when he wanted to he could rock the house. He was a 'big battery' and I loved him, as did a lot of people, so when he said he would come work for us I knew our forty-foot bar was too short!

Steven's expertise helped us out with managing the bar because Fred had no clue, only opinions. With the kitchen and bar coming together we started interviewing waitresses. During these interviews a young Dutch guy named Pele came and told us he wanted a job here no matter what and that he would do whatever necessary for no pay to learn. He was working near New York University in an ice cream store, but wanted to work at Fishbones because he loved what we were doing.

I'm not making this stuff up. Rather, I'm trying to show you that what I lacked in experience I could find in others and I did. For the opportunity to learn Jorge, Steven and Pele all gave us a lot in the beginning. I'll never forget that or them.

As it came together at Fishbones, the paper work out of Idaho began to get my attention. There was always something Mr. X wanted taken care of before he would send money. Every month we got interest statements and calls of great concern over every damn dollar, which really upset me. I was second-guessing my relationship with Mr. X already.

CHAPTER 10

Fine tuning all systems for take off

10. Fine Tuning All Systems for Takeoff

Paperwork

The last thing we want is to be burdened with forms. We did not put the effort and sacrifice into our project to wind up worrying about the piles of forms that can accumulate weekly, monthly and quarterly on our desk from all the different governmental agencies that kick in once we file incorporation papers. The amount of daily tracking forms that have to be dutifully recorded everyday can be overwhelming, but they are our in-house bookkeeping controls.

Once we've filled out the forms, the more complicated responsibilities have to be delegated to the right people, otherwise we'll be taken away from what we want to do and accomplish.

Our in house computer can do a lot to help with the bookkeeping that our accountant needs. User-friendly software for the restaurant business goes from $50 to complicated systems that cost thousands.

Our accountant has asked us to do our bookkeeping in Quicken, which costs under a $100. The nightly reports and daily deposits are recorded and everything that comes into our restaurant is paid for C.O.D. All liquor, food and assorted services are paid for upon delivery and recorded daily in Quicken. Every week, our checkbook, deposits and sales totals go to our accountant. The accountant then computes our payroll, and reconciles our bank balances and tax obligations.

Experienced restaurant accountants take care of the technical and complicated fiscal tax liabilities that even a Mom and Pop operation can incur. There are state, county and federal obligations that you never knew existed, as well as insurance obligations that vary according to the amount of business you do and how many employees you have. It's much better to let an accountant organize our taxes, payroll and insurance files because then we always submit what they need on time.

Hiring People

If we really think about hiring employees as an extension of ourselves, we can avoid a hundred mistakes that can be a never-ending source of disappointment. To casually hire anyone, whether a friend, relative or an off the street applicant, is an accident waiting to happen.

As firm as every step of the way has been to this point, we must further our resolve by hiring people we can train to do what needs to be done the way we want it done. And we must be wary of experienced restaurant people who try to sell themselves into our business. More often than not there's something screwy there.

1. Secure a detailed employment application. Read it and call *at least two* previous employers and references.
2. When we want to interview an applicant further, we'll do it together in a respectful manner, and:
    a. Keep it brief and to the point. To the point means getting a sense of the person's work ethic.
    b. All applicants hired must fill out INS I-9 forms, which are Employment Eligibility Verification papers. All employers need these forms completed and on file within three working days of hiring any individual.
    c. Find out about the applicant's personal life goals. Let them express themselves. If we interact in a meaningful way, we're on our way.
    d. Explain, in concise detail, what's expected of them, especially the dos and don'ts of our operation.

If they're okay with our two-week minimum wage training program prior to opening and we intuitively feel good about them, we should give them a try. If someone becomes problematic, well then, thank you very much. Next please!

Callous? Not at all! Where will we be in three weeks if we've hired a problem? Experience can quickly tell us: nowhere! Paolo and I both need people we can *train* and *count on*. It's not like we're building a pyramid, but it does become more and more apparent that the selection of each block in the building of our business deserves some very focused time. Clunkers, hustlers or malcontents, whether in the front or back of the house, can poison the whole effort and take the energy out of all of us. Casting is the most important element of our production and requires patient and tireless effort on our part.

It's sad to say, but in our present-day, multi-layered litigious society that we live in, the old way of doing business by making decisions on a handshake or someone's word is gone. Skilled hustlers make it much more risky and complicated. They can and do use federal and state agencies to falsely bring claims against you. For the cost of a phone call, they can have municipal departments all over your business checking out their unwarranted charges. So be forewarned. We'll try to keep it simple and hire only those we've thoroughly checked and feel can be trained to do what we want, the way we want it done. Because our staff is small, the moment we see a problem or a potential problem we can correct or resolve it immediately.

Losing loved ones is probably life's most painful blow. Losing at love is probably number two, but losing in business because trusted friends-employees are or were stealing from you can be totally devastating. Thieves and theft can only be eliminated by astute hiring practices and controls. What I want to get at here is a heightened awareness that is needed by all of us going into the restaurant business. Because when the doors open, our money, goods and property become easy targets for skilled thieves. A national business association that deals with employee fraud and theft estimates that the average daily dollar amount of employee theft in the mid-nineties is about ten dollars. The association's recommendations are very close to what we will follow here, but one phrase that caught my attention was: *Create a culture where theft is not a problem.*

In the old days, a saloon owner like my Uncle John would smash shut the cash register drawer. While the startled bartender counted his fingers, Monahan would roar, "That's my money lad, be careful with it!" Today there are point of sales computers and bar spotters that can be hired to watch bartenders. But none of these can stop a bartender from doing math in his head and taking the money when he finds the opportunity.

A friend of mine worked for years at a nearby culinary school. He told me the security force never watched the security monitors. Theft was a serious problem until the school put in airport-type security at the employee entrance-exit.

Basically, you can't stop theft, you can only control it. Many disgruntled employees steal because they figure you owe them more than they're getting. So they take a few bucks, a bottle of liquor, steaks, shrimp, and extra hours on their time cards. Many give away food and drinks to friends and family. No matter what, you lose.

When you lose food or drink you lose twice. First, you lose the cost of the product and then you lose the money that product would have generated as a sale. Help that steals, eats or ruins product can cost your business thousands of dollars each month.

Controlling this kind of behavior in Mom and Pop restaurants starts with double-checking on who you are hiring. Discussing the zero theft tolerance policy of our restaurant with the new employees sets the tone. Checks and balances include daily inventory control checklists for the front and the back of the house and time cards or sheets that must be checked nightly. Searching an employee's belongings goes too far, but watching them leave the restaurant after work *is* important. You can say thank you or goodnight while you check them out.

Paying employees fairly for the work they do and treating them well as individuals is very important. Empowered people—people who are appreciated for what they do—are much less likely to turn on you. Perks like a nice employee meal and an after work drink or dessert go a long way in telling your employees how you value them.

The Paid Enemy or The Employee from Hell!

A Different NYC Story

I've seen many people steal from mutual employers and I've caught some, though certainly not all, of the people who have stolen from my own businesses.

Personally, I got caught shop lifting M & Ms from Dreger's Market in my neighborhood when I was eight years old. The owner called my father at work. Later that day, when my father came home, I found myself being sent to the middle of next week via his belt and I had to go to confession. Father Austin gave me a penance of copying ten times each the dictionary pages featuring the words, stealing and thieves. After that I gave up M & Ms.

At my first job in the food service industry where I handled money, I watched my friend Kippy steal donuts and dollars from the donut shop we worked. The way I dealt with the situation was to find another job. Kippy was no longer a friend and I never went near that donut shop again, but I learned then that friends can steal and employers don't know what's going on if they're not there. Sadly my awareness of the real world had awakened.

What if that donut shop owner knew he was losing a lot of dough to theft and giveaways to the friends of his employees? He'd probably have Kippy in his office for a talk and I'd bet you ten dollars to a donut Kippy would blame me. So again, I knew it was wrong but more importantly I knew it happened and when I spotted it I would put some distance between thieves and myself over the years in this business.

I worked at the largest and busiest restaurant in New York City in the early eighties. The place employed hundreds and fed tens of thousands tourist diners a week. The gross and net sales were in the country's top five and at the time I was there their losses due to theft had to be at the top of the list.

Mother's Day in large restaurants can be the single highest grossing day of the year for a restaurant and it can also be the biggest day of the year for thieves. So it's Mother's Day 1981 at the restaurant where I work at as an expediter. The manager of the restaurant had an emergency and asked me to be a fill in as a Captain in the posh dining room. I used to work in the dining room but jumped at the opportunity to be an expediter.

So on Sunday I would work from nine in the morning till midnight. I'd make at least five hundred dollars in tips and the next time I needed time off or there were better expediting shifts available, the manager would take care of it for me.

The eight a.m. staff meal on Mother's Day was special. Dining room set ups were at nine a.m. and the first seating started at ten. I showed up around seven-thirty with my coffee and newspaper. I found a park bench behind the restaurant empty and settled in. About half way through my ritual a pickup truck backed up into the trash area and a couple of guys in grungy clothing jumped out of the truck and into the dumpster next to the truck and started rummaging through it. I had no idea or interest in what they were doing till I heard one of them yell something to the other one. I recognized that voice. The owner of that voice worked in the back of the house in the prep area. So I started watching what they were doing. They were unloading out of the dumpster coolers that took the two of them to lift. In a few minutes I saw them off load a dozen coolers into their truck. Then they left. Whatever was in the coolers was obviously perishable and carefully stored the night before in that dumpster.

And all of that was done in front of security guards and cameras unless the guards were partners or asleep and the cameras were off, broken or ignored.

So what could they be stealing? What do I care? I have to work a double today and I'm not a detective in the employ of the restaurant.

Fifteen minutes later I walked into the employee's restaurant entrance which was next to where purveyors also brought their goods to the back of the house receiving dock where they were checked in with the house buyer and receiver of goods. And what did I hear again? You're right! That voice was again telling his associate where to put the coolers on the receiving dock for inspection. Seeing this blew my mind. They were reselling what they stole the night before back to the restaurant on this busy day.

I saw that it was a lot of iced Red Snappers from Central America. Unbelievable!

I skipped the employee meal and went to my dining room station and made sure that I knew where everything was and what was needed. One by one my crew joined me. We were: me taking orders, a waitress getting all drinks, two back of the house waiters getting appetizers, salads, entrees, deserts and paying checks, and our fifty year old busboy. We all knew each other from various working stints together at this restaurant and we knew we were good to go to successfully get through this day and make some serious money. No slackers and we were a group that knew how to make the long day painless by helping each other out when needed.

The doors opened for business and long ago planned reservations filled our station immediately.

I put a rose in front of every mom and quickly took drink orders and chatted with family members and guests. Our team decided earlier that each one of us would tell each celebrating mom how nice she looked and how nice it was that they were all here. Bumping up the tip meter you bet! But also we all understood that just a few appropriate personal words on a special day like today could loosen the tightest purse and heartstrings.

The first seating ended with a lot of happy sons and daughters pressing tens and twenties into my goodbye handshakes.

The next seating was more demanding and the neighboring Captain was getting frazzled. He was complaining to me about everything, but I wasn't interested.

Our station got so busy that I had to go to the service bar for Champagne and glasses. While I was waiting my turn, I watched a bartender pocket cash from today's waiters for bottles of expensive champagne. He also did not key into the register my totals on our transaction. He was hustling, he was all over the back service bar like a human octopus, and I paid him. More on this later.

When I got back to my station one of my waiters said that the well-dressed couple standing in our station was talking nonsense and was dicey in his opinion so while I got rid of them he pointed them out to the floor manager and security. But the overwhelming frenzy of business let this team loose in the other dining rooms for about a half hour during which they stole fourteen wallets out of purses they lifted or cut from unsuspecting diners enjoying themselves.

The female would give the male the purse and he would lay it off to another woman who took the cash and credit cards out and then hid the purses where she could.

But one young man who's mother's and grand mother lost their purses was sharp enough to figure out what had happened and he chased the woman in to the ladies room and kept her there. He recovered a lot of people's valuables but not his mom's car keys as the police arrived. I mean it's not bad enough that thieves ruined these people's big day at the restaurant by stealing their money and credit cards but to leave these out of state visitors stranded without their car keys and house keys was a low blow.

Things ran smoothly through the lunch seating until two middle-aged sisters at a large party in another dining room had a drunken hair pulling fight to the cheers of other disgusted diners.

In the back of the house an out of control demanding waitress cut ahead in the expediter's line and yelled at Eddy she needed an order of:

"God-damn Eggs Sardou!" Her request went through the kitchen's microphone and one of the line cooks threw her order at her. In one minute Eddy had her out of the kitchen with the next in line waiter's Eggs Sardou and to the relief of everyone in the kitchen said into the microphone "the kitchen leads by one goal, let's rock!" He then gave the line the next order and had the train back on track.

A good expediter can control an even pace in large kitchens and also control the wait staff's behavior but he can't control where the food goes. So wait staff can put extra orders for themselves or others on a customer's order and later remove that off the bill.

A bad expediter can get anything from the kitchen for any wait staff he's in cahoots with. He can even outsmart a Point of Sales Computer if he has the time. He can also eat and drink whatever he wants via a grateful waiter or waitress.

The afternoon's business relaxed into a packed early evening's seating and some staff shift changes in the front and back of the house took place. We lost our bus boy and his replacement was related to the Captain in the station next to us that I mentioned earlier. I saw the two of them talking but he wasn't on the clock and still had time to eat so the rest of our crew took care of the filled station.

I suddenly realized that I forgot to get a new bundle of checks for the evening shift. When I had earlier turned in my book the new checks weren't ready. In the kitchen was the cashier cage that two people who processed all cash and charged checks for the entire restaurant. Each table in the restaurant had a slot on the wall that held the paid checks as they came in. Our new busboy was having a cashier process two different checks on two credit cards for his cousin the Captain next to us.

I looked up as the cashier put the processed checks into their slots. There were only a few checks in each slot and my eyes drifted over to my table's slots—they all contained four, five, six or more checks for each of our tables. As the cashier who I knew quite well gave me my new checks I asked him to let me see those checks just posted by my busboy. The box on each check that we are required to mark the time the party was seated had been written over on each check. I returned the checks and went back to my station.

The evening went as smooth as a crowded train wreck could go. I actually saw a waitress successfully perform the Heimlich maneuver on an over excited older mother who was choking. The woman's dentures came into our station along with a piece of prime rib. Our bus boy picked them up, rinsed and returned them. It was a very nice gesture, but I still knew he had been used by his Captain cousin to steal about $1200 dollars from the restaurant. How did the Captain's team do it?

On Mother's Day, very few people honoring their mothers look at their tab, a fact that an opportunistic thief knows all about. After a large party paid cash, they would hold the check and cash. When another similar party spent about the same amount and proffered their credit cards as family members do on special occasions, they would use that first check that paid cash again for this party. The people probably didn't even look at the check but signed the credit card. So the team pockets the cash and looks for the next opportunity and on a day like today they can get away with it. Basically, on holidays, cash is the way family members all chip-in and divide the dreaded check. By the Captain sending his unsuspecting cousin into the busy cashiers he stays away from causing suspicion and if later asked about lack of turnovers he can lie his way clear of any wrong doing.

Suddenly the kitchen doors blast open behind me and the restaurant security is pulling a sobbing, howling, and hysterical man into the kitchen with the restaurant manager and his assistants. Security says the young man is a professional con man who causes scenes like a bad actor till he's given money to get out of your place. Management thinks they need to help as the guy screams for his mother, the police, his medicine or whatever else comes to mind. The guy gets progressively worse as the minutes pass and somehow a woman claiming to be his mother is on the phone with the manager and the hysterical young man. They finish their scam and the manager pays out some money to the guy and he's gone. You wouldn't believe it if you saw it. Unbelievable! I returned to my station, thinking that guy is a good actor!

Name any celebrity favorite of yours and if they had a mother living in New York, they were at the last seating. They turned the dining room into a "stars under the stars" event. It was great to watch as they threw money around big time. I had to help get all the champagne bought for our station of, let's say, prominent Italian Businessmen. Back at the big service bar, the guy that was there earlier in the day as the human octopus selling his own champagne was gone. So I paid the bartender for my order and followed him with my eyes to the cash register and watched him correctly do our transaction. But wait a minute! Where's the cash register that the octopus was using all day? Gone. It was gone and I wonder how many others even noticed. I mean the guy brought his own register and champagne. To the restaurant's credit, they got him, but not until he had had a three-month run before being caught.

Mercifully, the day ended. We made a lot of money and headed for our hangout to unwind and talk about the crazy day at the glue factory with our co-workers. To be sure there were some more bizarre stories but the cash register caper pretty much had everyone's attention. I thought about all I'd seen that day, all that I missed, and I swore to never go into the restaurant business.

Enough said! Let's hire people correctly, train them properly and create a culture where theft is not our problem.

*   *   *

Employee Training

For the size of our restaurant, an employee manual would be a little excessive, but a two-page list of what's expected of our workers should be reviewed item by item with each employee. Their signature on the last page shows that they acknowledge and understand their job responsibilities.

Here is the list of responsibilities for our new floor staff at Tusculum's:

1. *Dress Code*: All floor staff will wear black shoes, black slacks, a white and clean dress shirt with no collar. The restaurant will pay half of their weekly laundry bill at the laundry around the corner. They must have two pairs of slacks and three shirts so they're always neatly dressed. Here again, the restaurant will split the costs with them and use a local merchant that will always stock that dress shirt.
2. *Personal Appearance*: All employees must take pride in their appearance and if we see a lack of pride, we'll point it out and have it corrected.
3. *Starting Time And Attitudes*: All floor staff employees will arrive for work at 4:00 P.M. every day of business. They'll sign in and do their side work. The employee meal will be served at 4:30 P.M. and Paolo and I will discuss different specials and new business during the meal. This is a great time to let the employees know how they're doing and for them to let us know where we can help them.

    All of our personal concerns are put on hold and the focus is put on the job ahead. It's a team meeting with a positive team spirit that makes the evening's dinner service so much easier and rewarding.
4. *Signing Out—Wages And Tips*: After the conclusion of dinner service and side work, the wait staff does their Check Control Sheet. On the Check Control Sheet they record the check number and the total dollar amount of their used checks. At the bottom of the Check Control Sheet is a box where they record the amount of their declared tips and another box that records the

time that they turned in the Check Control Sheet to me. The wait-staff has checked their checks, declared their tips and recorded time worked. All I have to do is double-check their figures. As you can see, the Check Control Sheet really works quite effectively.

Kitchen Employee Training

If a kitchen is the heart and soul of our restaurant, then the kitchen is also where our restaurant lives or dies. Our kitchen must produce quality product in a timely manner. This job—or art form—can only be performed by dedicated, experienced, and trained professionals who are paid accordingly.

Paolo and I know anything short of a well-trained kitchen staff, from Chef to dishwasher, line cooks to prep people, is certain death. Everyone in that room must know how and why things are done and hopefully the mix of people hired makes that room a great place to work. Paolo will work countless hours with his staff, training those that need to know the different tasks to be done day in and day out. Everyone has to know how to handle, prepare, cook and store food items according to local Health Department Regulations. Waste that is caused by the mishandling of foods is very costly. Health Department citations are even costlier. People who work in kitchens that don't know or like what they're doing, or don't pay attention to procedures, can sabotage the efforts of the kitchen and harm the hard earned reputation of a restaurant.

Have you ever thought about how much trust you put into each eating out experience? It's amazing that so few of us spend any time dwelling on who is making our meals. We put a lot of trust in our dining choices and over time we develop dining habits based on positive experiences. These positive experiences mainly have to do with always being satisfied with our meals. This means that our regular or favorite restaurant runs a tight kitchen and has trained personnel that take pride in consistently producing their product.

Our Money System

It's lucky our restaurant is two blocks away from three different banks with ATM machines because we are opening as a cash-only business and we've decided to not accept credit cards or personal checks. Why? We know a credit card company won't approve us because we have no track record. Also, we have no interest in giving 3-5% of our profits to credit card companies at this point.

Accepting personal checks from diners in any sizable city can be exasperating, disappointing and expensive. No checks accepted, no credit, and no tabs are good business choices for the obvious reasons.

Now that we've established we're a cash-only business, we can create a system to track the money:

1. Orders are taken on two-part guest checks. The server takes the first page to the kitchen to have the order filled. Drink orders are written on the back of the second page or hard check that the server keeps. After the customers complete their meals, the server gives them the totaled hard check. Clearly priced food, drinks and taxes are easily understood by the customer and payment is made to the server.
2. The server submits the check and payment to me at the bar where I enter each menu item, corresponding to preset keys on the cash register. The cash register provides a subtotal, automatically adds the tax, and totals the check. I return the check and any change to the server.

Cash registers with preprogrammed keys provide a detailed sales analysis and the collected sales tax total when zeroed out at closing time. These registers are a great control tool for limited-menu restaurants.

At the end of the evening, the servers reconcile their guest checks according to the check numbers used and totals collected on their Check Control Sheet. They then return to me the unused checks, which I reissue.

In a restaurant that's our size, the wait-staff pickup and deliver plates to each other's tables, so tips are pooled and evenly split. Good teamwork means better service and better service has its own rewards in the tips collected.

I then zero the register and take the tape, Check Control Sheets, checks and cash drawer downstairs, where I count the money, fill out the Daily Report, make out the deposit slips for our checking, payroll and tax accounts, rebuild the cash register bank, put everything in the safe, lock up the office and return upstairs.

The first thing to do when we return the next day is our banking. The benefit of daily banking and the recording or logging of our deposit slips for checking, payroll and tax accounts is that we know exactly where we stand everyday. By filling out our Daily Report and paying C.O.D. for every product or service we need, we know *exactly* where every penny comes and goes.

Most restaurant owners slowly become used to having employees sign for deliveries or repairs and services. But this is *slowly* the beginning of the end, when Daily Reports and deposits aren't organized money gets lost and the scramble to juggle all the requests for payment begins.

As this cycle runs its course, the tax account covers the other accounts. The taxes are postponed or ignored and once you get into the loop of receiving Notices for Payment from different tax agencies, you've pretty much shot yourself in the foot. The domino effect goes through the whole business and the doors are locked by either the landlord or the taxman, whoever gets there first.

It's so easy to do these simple chores that when I'm around people in this business who don't have a disciplined system, I can tell you exactly where they'll be in eighteen months.

When we finish the banking we should do the front and back of the house inventory and enter it in our Daily Report, day in and day out, every day of the year. This is how and where we control inventories. When we find things out of order, they can be easily corrected because every day they are checked.

If it turns out that taking credit cards is an absolute necessity in your restaurant I would strongly recommend you contact other local restaurants and find out their best credit card rates. The difference in points can save your business thousands of dollars a year.

Tusculum's Daily Report

DAY _____
SHIFT ☐ LUNCH ☐ DINNER

Prepared by _____
& Date

CUSTOMER AND	MON.	TUES.	WED.	THUR.	FRI.	SAT.	Begin. Invent.	Ending Invent.	Weeks Total	Last Week	Month To Date
MEAL TOTALS											
Checked Sales											
FOOD											
BEER											
WINE											
SODAS											
TOTAL SALES											
TOTAL SALES TAX											
LABOR - WAGES											
Purchases											
Food											
Wine											
Beer											
WATERS - SODAS											
Total Purchases											
Weekly Rent											
Fixed Expenses											
Sales Tax dep.											
Payroll dep.											
Checking dep.											
Savings dep.											

Our Daily Report

Our Daily Report

Our daily report can be as complex as a VCR manual or as simple as managing your checkbook. This is a *very critical* part of our daily operational procedure. We use this report to control theft, food and liquor inventories, and labor costs. Again, it's another aspect of a daily discipline that needs to be performed so we know at all times *exactly* where every dollar is.

The daily report allows us to crosscheck our wait-staff Check Control Sheet system with Paolo's kitchen totals. Both of these reports are checked against my zeroed out register tape. On the tape, as on most electronic cash registers are PLUs, Price Look Up Key codes. PLUs on the zeroed out tape give every item purchased by a corresponding menu item number. This simple control system works efficiently, takes minutes to do, and can further manage our costs when we enter this data onto our Daily Report.

Essentially, **Dollars-In** are tracked this way:

1. Wait-staff records the order for the kitchen and bar on a two-copy check system. The kitchen fills the orders and retains their checks.
2. Beer, wine and sodas are checked off the wait-staff checks by the bartender when drinks are served.
3. At end of dining, the customer receives their check and the money is paid. The bar/house register records the sale by entering each item sold via the corresponding menu item number system.
4. At end of the business day the wait-staff checks are double-checked by the back and front of the house off their Check Control Sheet.
5. Tape is zeroed out and sales are recorded by departments on the tape. Food, wine, beer, sodas and sales tax are all broken down for us on the tape.

6. The data is entered on our Daily Report and the zeroed out tape is stapled to it.
7. Deposit slips are filled out, recorded on a deposit tracking form and taken to the bank.

We now know what's in the bank. We know what's been used and what's needed for the front and back of the house inventories. Also, we are monitoring our payroll obligation.

Hopefully, this exercise gives us all a sense of being in control of our production. Without systems like our Check Control Sheet and Daily Report, systematically used every day, we're lost at sea without charts, heading directly towards the rocky shores of the restaurant graveyard.

As we did with the floor plans in the previous chapter we'll now draw up Tusculum's Daily Report.

Our Daily report is pretty self explanatory and very well suited to our operation. The day before we open, all inventories are recorded. The morning after our first night of business, we begin the daily practice of recording current inventories. I like to estimate the daily wages earned by our employees and cover them with a daily payroll deposit. Since we are a C.O.D. restaurant, we record all purchases paid out daily.

We broke down our monthly rent and fixed expenses into weekly figures so we can monitor them and make sure our checking account balance covers them at the end of the month. While doing this math, we added wages in with the rent and utilities. We then were able to come up with an average year-round hourly cost of running our restaurant. That figure, which is based on being open five hours a night, six nights a week, is close to $135.00 an hour. This is the cost of opening our doors nightly, utility consumption, staff, rent, insurance, licensing and in-house emergencies (power outages or other loss of business) in New York City, 2000.

To further explain this rocket science report let me give you a little of my uncle John's advice from his Monahan's Full House. "Ya gotta get to your place early, because from the time ya left it last night somethin' happened. Everyday it's always the devil messin' in my workshop. Bless them lazy Saints, the devil ain't burnt me out and back to Ireland." In this business, no matter on what level your operating, it's always something!

It makes a great deal of sense to know what our fixed expenses are at any time. It helps to make sure that the hours we are open generate enough business to cover these expenses. That's why our Daily Report is a very helpful tool and a must-do daily discipline.

My N.Y.C. Story Part 7

THE FEAR OF PAINFUL DECISIONS

We were ready on some levels to open Fishbones in the dead of winter 1985. What I felt would happen happened really quickly. The curtain went up and all the main characters performed well. For that effort, I was very gratified, because if I hadn't made sure that those specific people I mentioned earlier on were hired, we would've been dead in the water.

I used to think that working in restaurants was hard. Owning restaurants and making them work is another story. Doing it with partners that you not only have to lead, but also include in the decision-making process from hiring the right personnel, managing the floor, monitoring food and liquor costs to creating or designing a menu, and then getting them to see it your way is like performing brain surgery with garden tools.

When success comes to visit your efforts, you need a person who can take charge and make it all work. Dead weight has to be bagged and put out with the garbage. Your success is equal to the effort you make in maintaining the consistency of the product delivered. The result of working in a strained partnership is worse than dentistry without X-rays and drugs. And this is exactly where *consistency* falls off and the business suffers.

What I'm getting at is that my partner Fred was a dud and there's no way to change that now. But when you truly know *what you want*, then getting into uncomfortable and confrontational situations with people does not stop you from making necessary changes. Instead of getting rid of Fred from the beginning, I suffered the fool. Partly because of Dylan and partly because of his $25,000 and his start-up sweat equity, but mainly because I wasn't one hundred percent clear on knowing what I wanted.

Timing is everything in life and as winter ended and spring sprung, our Californian-style bar and restaurant started rocking big time. Steven, Nancy, Donnie, Lisa, John, Danny and Libby rocked the house out front. In the kitchen, Jorge and his crew sent 100 to 200 plates of healthy and hearty Cal-Mex food every night in a 50-seat dining room.

We were beginning to make *burning down the house numbers*. But to do those numbers takes a toll.

I'm a big battery kind of worker and I only ask that those I'm working with as partners do the same. When they don't, resentment starts its acidic juices flowing and soon enough, enough is enough!

Coming into summer, we were one of the hottest tickets in town. I'm very proud of that and am quick to give credit where its due: Steven and his crew, Jorge and his people, the great women who staffed the dining room and Pele the runner who carried plates up and down stairs all night long. They all had a great work ethic and, because we were so busy, it was fun making money in a rockin' place. The artwork by Eric Brown had great whimsy and the sum total of all these efforts made the production work seemingly effortlessly because we were delivering the *feel good* product. From this idea that I originally had, we built a staff, made great food, served fun drinks, sold cool shirts, hats, glasses and delivered a good time.

By the middle of summer we had more staff, longer hours and all the business we could handle. People loved Fishbones. It was a thing of beauty and a lot of fun—except for Fred.

I now understand that people who are creative and talented have an obligation to those gifts. We have to use those talents and creativity in rewarding ways. We also have to protect these gifts from those who have none and try to dismiss or destroy ours.

Without question, I was the creative force behind the Fishbones look, style, and vibe. I had put together a great staff with a few minor problems and I also knew a lot of people who supported us in the beginning. I enjoyed meeting new customers, making new friends, cheerleading the staff and putting in the long hours. It was all very natural to me and I was comfortable in my role as team leader in the beginning. Slowly I began to notice that the buddy-buddy relationship we shared during the building of Fishbones was changing. Dylan's background was as a builder and Fred's was much the same; the job they did was well done. But builders of restaurants are not ready or capable of running a restaurant.

Many business people tend to hustle anyone who'll listen to them. A successful one will make a deal with someone who has a lot on the ball. But good business people or hustling shysters can only help open a restaurant. They can't run it or help with the day-to-day difficulties of the business. They can only mess with bottom line details that consume them. Borrowing money is a very upsetting experience when the lender starts telling you how to better run the business that he invested in because of you.

We were six months old when what I was getting from the investor and the dud partner was wearing thin. Both of them wanted an equal share in the profits and neither was doing anything near what Dylan and I were putting into the production. Doomsday was looming because we finally started listening to the wake up call we were getting everyday.

Running a restaurant demands a lot out of qualified people; to the unqualified, it demands they learn their craft by working hard and observing. Dylan did that. He worked hard and learned everything I knew. He appreciated what I did as much as I appreciated what I learned from him. Neither Fred nor the investor put in an effort equal to ours. Instead, these two always came up with self-serving opinions, criticism, negativity and stupid ideas about money. My playing into their greed and neuroses started coming up short as the place was making more and more demands on Dylan and me. Twelve-hour days rolled into sixteen-hour days and boozy nights. It was getting to be too much for Dylan and me, so one day I crossed the partner-friendship line and told Dylan that if he agreed, we should bump Fred and Mr. X the investor because they were both problematic.

He agreed. We decided to pay off our loan before confronting Mr. X, but Fred had to go. We picked a date in the fall to deal with Fred so we could get though the summer.

As fall was approaching Fishbones was seriously busy and Fred was becoming more insufferable by the day. He was causing more and more problems with his laziness, bias, prejudices, and politically incorrect stupidity, so Dylan and I moved the confrontation date to right after the Labor Day weekend.

We all met at 10:00 a.m. at Fishbones. We sat at the bar with our coffee, attempting small talk. I let Dylan lead the conversation into the topic that was burning us to the quick. As soon as Dylan started in with criticism of Fred's work ethic and his lack of respect for ours, Fred began crying and saying things like: "I never knew I'd lose my best friend in a business deal that I brought him into. You're closer to Dylan than I've ever been. You've got what I always wanted, his respect. I can change. I can make it up to you guys. Give me another six months and if it doesn't work, I'll leave."

When Dracula is writhing in the sunlight begging for forgiveness, we all want the hero to drive the stake into and through his heart. But somehow the human frailties of our hearts always trick us and the hero into backing off. The monster continues to live, causing havoc and destroying lives.

When we know what we want, we can drive the stake through the heart of any obstacle that deters us from our game plan and goals. I didn't do it that day and it cost me a lot. Maybe it cost Dylan more, because they were longtime friends, but the whining act and the self-serving tears screwed up the next few years of our business and lives. We gave him a second chance instead of dealing with the pain, bad feelings and the expense of divorcing ourselves from him. To this day I always go back to that scene in my mind and cringe. Fishbones got busier and busier and Fred made an effort to put in more hours, but couldn't change or even get out of his own way, so nothing really changed except that he had more time on the job to screw things up. And he did.

CHAPTER 11

Rehearsal Week

11. The Rehearsal Week

Every human endeavor that succeeds is tirelessly rehearsed. From Broadway to Hollywood and Vine, from delicate surgery to sports, from the Arts to the War Rooms, practice and rehearsal run-throughs prepare us to execute and perform our tasks.

Why a week? Because that's what it'll take to bring our staff around to seeing things our way and for them to be comfortable with us before we open and are ready to succeed.

Restaurants, like all Arts, are subject to criticism, whether it's word of mouth or printed reviews. This is a survival reality check in our business and we're preparing ourselves for good word of mouth reviews in our chosen neighborhood. A good or great printed review would be a bonus, but not what we're after here. The sub-text of our rehearsal week goes something like this: *If you don't have it right to start, don't bother!*

During rehearsal week, the floor staff will see each menu item prepared by Paolo and crew. They will taste test all of the menu items as well as the featured wines. If we've done our homework and successfully hired the right and willing floor staff they will be well compensated for their training time on their first week's check.

Paolo and I always have to remind each other to be as patient and informative as we can be during this stage of production, because if we succeed at including all of our people in a family-like mix, our jobs are going to be much more enjoyable and personally rewarding.

It doesn't take more effort to train people in an environment where they know and understand that they're part of what we're doing and that they are appreciated and needed than it does to threaten them with stupid rules and attitudes.

Being candid with employees about our financial responsibilities and obligations lets everyone share in the bottom line reality of what we each have to provide to succeed.

It's not just another job! It has meaning and purpose for all of us. If we sink together in the same direction, so be it. If we succeed in pulling the train in the same direction, we'll all share in the success. Paolo and I believe in Christmas bonuses where we can demonstrate our appreciation when it's really needed.

Back to the rehearsal: I show points of service over and over again. Our greeting at the seated table is: "Welcome to Tusculum. Our special tonight is dadada…and the suggested wine is dadada. Would anyone care for something to drink?"

The bus person sets the warm bread and olive oil on the table, opens the large bottle of mineral water, and pours the water into glasses of ice cubes and a lemon slice.

After drinks are served and partly enjoyed, orders will be taken and posted. All plates of food are served to the right side of the customer by all floor staff. Plates are cleared from the left. All dining room staff always keep each other to their right side no matter what direction they're going in. This simple traffic awareness lets everyone know where they should be and avoids costly collisions. Banging into each other and dropping orders is such an aggravating and expensive problem that I demonstrate it daily.

Losing plates screws up the dining room and kitchen. The event really upsets the dining experience of a customer missing a meal while his friends eat their meal.

Next we go over and over how orders are written for accuracy and clarity. All orders have numbers and if something additional is required, it is clearly printed and never written for the kitchen. Paolo and crew will have such pressure on themselves to handle nightly dinners that unreadable orders are worse than sand in your mouth. It takes the kitchen out of sync, makes tempers flare, wastes time and costs us money.

At the wait-staff station we have an area for writing and adding up check totals. The calculator gives them a tape with the totals that they staple to the customer's check. They also have in their station sweet Amaretto cookies that go to the table with the check.

As mentioned previously, check writing ends with the wait-staff doing their end-of-service Check Control Sheet, returning unused checks, tip declarations, side work completed and checked off. The last and very important detail is the signing out time and total daily time worked recorded on the same sheet. Tipping is their business and responsibility, but we have to collect this information for our accountant. Controlling overhead is vital to the health of our business. Lapsing into a casual approach slowly snowballs into costly mistakes.

Control is not the buzzword of the restaurant business. It is the *buzz saw* of the restaurant business. When there are so many variables that must be optimally performed, it's our control systems that correctly guide our many efforts.

"We do it to succeed. If we don't, we fail!"

That's what God must have told Ray Kroc one night because look at the success of MacDonald's simple systems. When problems arise, we can usually find the answers easily. Either the system is not being used correctly or it's been violated. That's when the buzz saw starts up.

In the middle of Rehearsal Week we can tell if our staff is getting the big picture or not. If we're happy with the results, we invite all of them and their guests to dinner at Tusculum. In this setting we can show them the experience we want our customers to experience when they're working and they're in charge. *In Charge* is a big subject, but one I want to address while the staff are our guests.

Paolo and I outlined and planned for this moment throughout our relationship. How are we both going to get our people to gel and perform?

We've put a lot of thinking and effort into the employee as guest dinner, knowing we'll find the effort well rewarded. At this meal where we serve the people we've hired, we are taking it one step further. *We are going to empower them and give them authority.* This evolves from the idea of a family-run Mom and Pop philosophy: We show we have real trust and respect in their abilities to professionally handle their parts in our production. As working owners, we will back them up one hundred percent because they're part of our extended family.

When our employees are working a section of our restaurant, in actuality they are In Charge of that part of the world we've created at Tusculum. They know and understand their range of authority and make the same decisions Paolo or I would.

This is the point in their training where we want them to seize empowerment and understand that it is essential to their success. Like us, they need to know and understand what acceptable behavior is and is not.

Effective leadership requires a passion for doing your job well. That feeds your character a sense of integrity so you know what's right and what's wrong. In our little world, we run a tight ship on our terms. The myth of "the customer is always right" is archaic and not applicable to our restaurant in the here and now.

After price, the most desired customer need is: "Make it easy for me. Tell me what I want." This is what our empowered staff does with their expertise. They guide our customers through a rewarding dining experience. When a customer causes a problem, our empowered staff is trained to understand what was said—or demanded—and then *they* decide on what needs to be done. They are In Charge and have an awareness of what's possible and what's not at any point in time.

Some examples of *what's not acceptable*:

1. Rudeness, drunkenness, or lewdness.
2. Any type of hostility or abusive behavior toward any of our staff.

3. Loudness or profanity that disturbs other customers.
4. Obnoxious, misbehaving children.
5. Menu changes or price changes.
6. Plate splitting and demands for extras.

In this business, 99% of your customers are happy with value for their dollar, served with a friendly hello and goodbye. But there's always that one percent of problematic customers who, if not kept in check, can ruin the night for everyone. They upset or offend our well-meaning staff with their inappropriate behavior and demands.

Customer satisfaction is what good businesses build repeat business on and that is what we're all trying to do. In the restaurant business, people are not buying cars; they're having a meal. If they have a problem with our product without question our staff will respond with: "How can we make this situation work for you?" If people abuse our customer satisfaction policy, our staff can pick up their check and direct them to me. I'll listen, support my staff and discourage these people from returning.

In almost every restaurant I ever worked or dined in, the un-empowered staff would suffer through unpleasant experiences on the floor and then unload those feelings on other co-workers in the kitchen, upsetting the whole house. The management or person in charge also bit the bullet because they all were shackled with the myth that the customer is always right.

But when one of our empowered employees confronts a problematic customer with "No, that's not possible," or "Your behavior is not acceptable here and you'll have to leave," the customer will either comply or demand to see the manager or owner. When we support our employee and tell the customer the same thing, the problem is ended, feelings aren't hurt and we can continue. Empowerment is a responsibility, but you'll be amazed at the amount of energy and excitement it gives your employees.

Paolo and I join our empowered staff for dessert at the end of the employee as guest dinner. We ask for their feed back in any areas they are not comfortable with, because the full dress rehearsal is two nights away and opening night is three nights away. Here, again, you'll be amazed at what an empowered staff can do. Before they knew how much we valued them and trusted in their abilities, they would have edited their feedback and opinions to please us. They would have hidden their doubts, questions and fears. Empowered employees test you right away and go right to their problem areas, state their problem and wait to see how you're going to handle it. I've found that we can best solve these problems by play-acting the scene out for the employee, because, although we know the answers, we can best show them the solution with humor and insight by acting it out. Paolo and I both are big hams, so the group enjoys seeing that side of us and we enjoy getting the points across.

In this informal dinner meeting, a lot has been accomplished toward making the family-like mix a reality. Paolo and I talked through the cleaning up after our guests had left, about how it was coming together and how right it felt.

The following rehearsal day we had a lively staff eagerly waiting to get to the business at hand. They were proudly dressed in their new uniforms and ready. We got some good feed back and good questions that they had obviously slept on. One question that everyone wanted answered was: Why doesn't the restaurant have a phone? I showed them a Tusculum business card that had our pay phone number on it and explained that a phone system for a restaurant our size was a time-wasting, expensive distraction. We don't take reservations and, for that matter, we only seat large tables when the whole party is in attendance.

The biggest telephone time waster is sales people trying to sell us everything imaginable. We're not interested, because we only buy what we need when we need it.

Since the staff was dressed for service I told them they would be serving lunch to our guest speaker. We again went over the menu item by item, wrote up and totaled out numerous checks. At lunchtime our friend Carol Matthews, the wine expert, poured all the wines from our menu for the staff to taste and learn a little about. She also showed the staff how to open and pour a glass of wine. Carol, who's a great lover of Italian food, soon was exchanging ideas and information with the staff and she gave Paolo's lunch fare two thumbs up. The following is Carol's wine list for the restaurant and our costs and profit on each bottle and glass served.

WHITE WINES

- Pinot Grigio, produced by Cavit from the Friuli region. Fresh in aroma and flavor, light in body and texture. Our cost $6.59; we sell it for $14 a bottle, $3.50 a glass.
- Pinot Grigio, by Zamo+Zamo from the Friuli region. Bold fruit and nutty flavors, crisp and clean, with a refreshing balance and taste. Our cost $11.49; we sell for $24 a bottle, $6.00 a glass.
- Pinot Grigio, by Santa Margherita, from the Friuli region. Light lemony taste, zesty and clean, very classy. Our cost $12.69; we sell for $26 a bottle, $6.00 a glass.
- Orvieto Seco, by Vaselli from the Umbria region. Rarely perfectly dry, just the right balance of fruit against a faintly tart aftertaste, very pleasing. Our cost $5.82; we sell for $12.00 a bottle, $3.00 a glass.
- Greco Di Tufo, By Feudi Di San Gregorio from Campania. Dry white with beautiful golden yellow color. One of Italy's finest whites, very pure fruit flavors with a crisp style and hint of toasted almonds. Our cost $10.16; we sell for $20.00 a bottle, $ 5.00 a glass.

RED WINES

- Sangiovese, by Antinori Santa Christina from Toscana. Smooth, soft fruit flavors, very versatile with food and very easy to drink. Our cost $6.98—we sell for $14.00 a bottle—$3.50 a glass.
- Salice Salento, by Cosimo Taurino from the Puglia region. Deep, rich earthy aromas and flavors, very expansive on the palate and very mouth filling. Our cost $6.82; we sell for $14.00 a bottle, $3.50 a glass.
- Chianti Classico, by Badia A Colti Buono from Toscana. Dry, well rounded ruby red wine from primarily Sangoviese grapes, velvety with beautiful graceful balance. Our cost $10.16; we sell for $21.00 a bottle, $5.00 a glass.
- Amarone, produced by Zenato, from the Veneto region. Great texture, rich and concentrated very assertive, with deep layers of dried fruits and spice. This wine also has intense earthy aromas and flavors in the finish. Our cost $20.16; we only sell by the bottle for $36.00.

SPARKLING

- Prosecco Di Valdobbiadene, by Brut Zardetto from the Veneto. Fresh fruity flavors, light and frothy, a very tasty elegant bubbly. Our cost $8.82; we sell for $20.00 a bottle, not by the glass.

Carol also selected a house red wine that would be served in pitchers. Our per-ounce costs are less than half of any bottled wine—"a glass of wine that makes the house a long buck." Carol's insights and generous expertise hit home with the staff. They're informed and excited about now being able to help customers make the best selections to go along with their dinner choices. The company that imports all the above selections is: WINEBOW Inc. 1-800-445-0620.

After lunch we showed all our employees where the restaurant electrical power panel was located. I explained what each labeled switch did and had them all flip the switches. Then we found every fire extinguisher in the restaurant and showed everyone how to use them. Next we went to the large first-aid kit and went through the use of each item in it. Finally and because I used it and have seen it used, we rehearsed the Heimlich maneuver for choking victims.

Like a play's director after watching a rehearsal, I went over some notes with our staff and answered more questions. They're ready and we're ready for the full dress run-through tomorrow night. We'll all meet for lunch at another neighborhood restaurant tomorrow.

Paolo and I had invited 40 friends and family for the rehearsal dinner. We decided on a four-item menu with soup and dessert. The wait staff successfully informed, guided and served the guests a great meal complemented with a terrific glass of wine. The checks were done correctly and logged onto their Check Control Sheets and I actually did a Daily Report later with Paolo. The production worked without a hitch. Mundane as these steps must sometimes seem, I can promise you that from where we're sitting looking at our opening night is very satisfying because our whole cast is rehearsed and waiting for the curtain to go up.

Anything short of this type of effort will be terminal within eighteen months. I know this to be true. I've been there and done that. Succeeding is better!

As redundant as this rehearsal week might seem to some of you the alternative is worse. The couple of thousand dollars it cost to have everyone in our production knowing what they're doing is nothing; it'll come back ten-fold. For all of us to be aware of what we're doing all of the time puts us in the moment. When we're in that moment, we are focused and perform to the best of our abilities.

We were ready the next night for our opening and it went very well. We served 81 dinners on a drizzly damp night with a World Series game on network TV.

The wait staff had no major problems and I can see we're going to need more help very soon. It's the same thing at Paolo's end. When the place fills up and the wait-staff holds orders trying to take other orders, the kitchen can easily get buried. Tomorrow at the staff meal we'll tell the staff to post each order before taking another. Paolo then will have one of his guys only doing appetizers and salads and putting them up in the pickup window away from the entrees that Paolo is putting in the pickup window. During the rush there was confusion. Orders were mixed up in the pickup window mainly because of the volume of plates all trying to go out of the same place. The problem was easily corrected and Paolo would call someone in the next day to do the new salad-appetizer station.

We signed out everyone, did our paper work, locked the doors, and we went out for drinks up the street. We watched the end of the World Series Game, but all we talked about was how well the first night had gone. It was a great night for us. It was just like winning the World Series.

My N.Y.C. Story Part 8

TAKE YOUR EYES OFF THE ROAD
AND SOONER OR LATER, BAM!

What was coming to a head at Fishbones was a crash course in how to best mishandle success. Grow-up school prepares few of us for success because very few of us really prepare ourselves to succeed. Knowing what you really want and how to go about getting it prepares you for anything.

Here I am, a year later, in a completely different situation than my Mister Chicken disaster. Even though I knew a lot about what I wanted and what I wanted Fishbones to be, I wasn't prepared for all the office work and more importantly I didn't want anyone else to do it! So, because I had a little knowledge of what needed to be done, I asked around and got an accountant's number and called him. We were busy and working late and partying too much, so we let this guy screw us around for about six months. I couldn't even stand to look at the guy or be in the same room with him. He wasn't big on personnel hygiene, he chain-smoked and I could never understand clearly what he was doing. Sad to say he took ill and I replaced him with a slick high-flying accounting firm that appeased Mr. X but drove me closer to going nuts.

We weren't computerized and we weren't accounting sophisticated, but we were busy and could afford these guys who placated Mr. X's obsession with counting money. So it began with Mr. X getting reports from these accountants and him calling them up and the two of them calling us with questions. Because Mr. X was owed money, we had to kowtow to these bean-counter grillings.

Then I realized that at Fishbones I had more support from the people I hired than from the partners I was in bed with, except for Dylan. I became much more assertive with those partners and replaced the high-flying pricey accountants with a younger flat-fee firm that educated me in a lot of accounting areas. The most important lesson that I learned from them was that I never should have made the deal with Mr. X in the beginning. And they had ways to get me out of it with other money at a much cheaper price.

This firm also thought they could find the financing to bump Fred out of the deal. With all their restaurant experience they quickly saw Mr. X and Fred as two problems that were legally tied into a business with unlimited potential.

Flattery is a tricky drug. On the one hand, earnest accountants are giving me the right advice and on the other hand the business is jumping and realtors and developers who are looking for clients are hustling us with deals from all over the country, blowing our egos up into insufferable numbskull delirium. Because I didn't know what I really wanted and wasn't prepared for the handling of success, I went with the least painful choice.

Here we are with a growing business that should be our total focus and we're being distracted by all these outside hustlers looking to get some part of what we're doing that works for them—and we're listening to them. In hindsight, that was faulty thinking, because I started dreaming about more restaurants instead of following the advice of the accountants.

By the end of our first year in business we had paid back Mr. X with interest and he was now a participating partner in the net profits. He continued to hassle the accountants for weekly statements and then always hammered us about his suspicions. Yet, because he helped me when I had nothing but an idea, I thought he should do the next one with us. If he went with us, then Fred would be included also. As I type this, I ask myself, what kind of business decision is that? Dumb to be sure, but one I've never made since.

When you're busy in New York City you're really busy and it's heady stuff when people enjoy what you've done. So you spend more money to improve or enlarge the place and you hire more people. Then you commit your first irreversible sin: you make someone a manager of your business so you can have a life. Then you listen to your manager sell you on computerizing your business and because that person is now in the office on the computer that same manager sells you on the idea of having a floor manager.

Hiring managers is a grievous mistake, in my opinion, because seldom does a great one appear that justifies your decision to let someone else run your business and count your money, let alone deserve their pay demands. At Fishbones we had these managers that were well paid by us and *managed* by me. But because business was so strong, they looked great. So I overlooked their mistakes, tolerated their naive ideas for creating more jobs, and told them the systems we created would handle their problems because I wanted to open more stores. I couldn't do anything if I was chained to Fishbones for 16 hours a day.

I wanted to create new places and put together the people to run them and then be onto the next one. *That's what I really wanted to do.* I just didn't know how to go about it without the people I was obligated to at Fishbones. I was always getting distracted with this desire to do more. Then I decided to begin looking for the next location which took me, and later us, away from the success we had into a big mistake.

Our management at Fishbones was earnest, hard working, expensive and inexperienced. While they were learning their craft they hired some clunkers and bad apples. And while the cats were working away somewhere else, the mice played.

Fishbones started out as a Mom and Pop place by which I mean we built it and operated it and any time that changes problems follow. Whatever I was doing elsewhere was always interrupted by problems at Fishbones. I'd go back and go nuts, fire the problem, cause other ones by working there again, and neuter all the efforts of our earnest management staff.

Luckily the business continued to grow and profit in spite of our many mistakes. I think we all fed off of an unbelievable stroke of luck: We were a rocking Upper West Side place where people wanted to go in the 1980s when the economy was raging and yuppies wanted to party.

I won't bore you with the details, but the busier we got the more volatile Fishbones became. Just keeping up with the business of running this busy business was overwhelming. We had NFL rejects as doormen, letting one customer in and one out until four a.m. on busy weekends. We were prey to every hustler and thief known to man, from pickpocket teams and a greedy landlord to nasty scary characters off the street. A lot of our partying customers would get carried out and put in cabs after we introduced over-proof Jell-O shots to New York City. Rowdy customers and problems were quickly and decisively handled and we continued to pour.

Through all of this chaos the one constant that I fought hardest to control and protect was Jorge and his crew in the kitchen. They did an amazingly thankless job. When I wasn't around, Fred or a manager would mess with them and the menu. But Jorge and I always survived their nonsense with my barking at them. The menu stayed the same and Jorge and his crew got raises.

The actor-chef got his walking papers. Jorge made some personnel changes and ran the whole show. He did the work schedules, ordered the food and delivered food costs that were terrific. I never understood why my partners never saw the beauty of our kitchen until I finally realized that none of my partners were experienced restaurant people who could appreciate the work ethic of Jorge and his crew. On that level alone, I should have learned something about doing business with these people, but I didn't. Can you tell me why I continued in this direction? If you can't, read no further, because you've missed the point. You've let go of the wheel and are headed for the same disaster I experienced.

CHAPTER 12

I.R.S. ~ I Rest Soundly

12. I.R.S.—I Rest Soundly

Be honest, work hard and the bottom line falls into place. In this chapter it is imperative that we take these business principles to heart and understand that operators who steal, hide and connive tax-cheating schemes suffer more than those of us who pay. A friend of mine once said "the man who thinks about his death dies a millions times." Chiseling the state and local governments out of sales taxes and the federal government out of various other taxes gets you thinking about what you'll do when you get caught a million times. The *getting caught fears* flow into sleepless nights, which wastes too much precious time and energy.

Mom and Pop owner-operators know full well that taxes are a reality they have to work with and that worry is the interest paid by a troubled mind and a troubled mind is bad for their business.

The various government agencies we all have to deal with are now becoming connected in cyberspace and are more cunning and sophisticated by the minute. It's the world we live in and the rules are simply part of the game we want to work and play in. If you want to take on the different government agencies to steal a buck, get into something else, because there's hardly enough time left over in the restaurant business to have a life, let alone enough time to figure how to stay out of debtor's prison.

The uses of all the new technologies to collect what's owed are relentless. Once you've not complied correctly with any of the above-mentioned agencies your whole world turns upside down. Even if it is an honest oversight, the struggle and frustration to correct it is maddening.

It's maddening to try and get your world right side up. Why? Because the burden of truth is now your responsibility and because these different agencies' letters, demands and actions are so intimidating we have to seek legal expertise and that does not come cheaply.

So who wins? Well, of course, they do. But no matter what the outcome, the time, money and energy wasted far outweigh whatever we hoped to gain. That's what different governmental agencies can do. Disgruntled customers and employees can activate them with complaints and documentation unbeknownst to you. The way to protect yourself, business and family is quite simple: be honest, enjoy your hard work, and be happy in your life away from the restaurant.

Most important, you have to have an on-going business relationship with an accountant who has extensive restaurant expertise. Through weekly communications you can both work on the necessary financial needs and obligations of your restaurant's business.

Another area of great concern for any restaurant owner is his insurance coverage. Is the replacement amount of insurance you carry enough to replace the building if you lost it in a fire? Do you have adequate business interruption coverage if anything terrible happens? Can you prove to the insurance company in your claim what you lost? You can, if you have in a safe place other than the restaurant, a detailed inventory, photographs, receipts and a videotape of everything. Insurance companies now require burdens of proof from all policyholders. If you don't have proof you may not get paid. It will take a bit of your time to document your business property, but you'll never lose sleep over having done it.

Another big issue that few businesses have any idea about, but one that is definitely a restaurant task that must be done and on file, is the I-9 form required by the Immigration and Naturalization Service for each of your employees. The INS I-9 form is each new employee's Employment Eligibility Verification that has to be on file three days after hiring the individual. Employer's must review, verify and sign these forms. No matter what anyone tells you about these forms, the law simply states that any business in the U.S. that employs one or more individuals must have the I-9s on file. The fines that the INS can give you are significant and they can remove illegal employees and shut down your business.

*******My N.Y.C. Story Part 9*******

HOW EVERYTHING SO RIGHT WENT WRONG!

The success I was experiencing at Fishbones was only in dollars. All of a sudden, there were lots of dollars. The dollars made my relationship with Fred and Mr. X more tolerable, but the rash never went away. So Dylan and I opted to do more because we weren't strong enough to deal with a big and unpleasant business divorce. Dylan and Fred also met and married women whom they met at Fishbones. Soon enough they were expecting and moving out of the city.

The next restaurant ran way over budget in another Upper West Side location near Columbia University. We opened Roosters successfully and had a great year. Now I ask you to read the previous sentences again and tell me from what we've learned and done together in this book, what's wrong with this picture?

1. Making money is fine when you enjoy how you're making it. I wasn't happy because I knew what I wanted and was afraid to walk away from not only the money, but also the rush of making it in the Big City.
2. Avoiding painful business decisions when you know things are wrong only lets the inevitable big ugly confrontation become more scary and intimidating.
3. My partner's marriages brought two new opinions to every meeting we had. The arrival of babies also required that the fathers be home at night. Our restaurants had to be run by less

than honest managers, opportunistic bartenders and very under trained wait-staff.

4. The budget over-run certainly thrilled Mr. X. Fishbones secured his loan and interest rates were rising. We had a great first year and retired some principle. But the interest alone on $250,000 each month buries you and continues to accrue. If you honestly look at the debt, interest and your overhead versus your gross, you have 250,000 reasons for grave concern.

5. Jorge ran both kitchens and always kept me informed of the stupid things Fred was doing, and what was going wrong with the managers and wait staff. He felt that Roosters needed me there full time in the same way that we started Fishbones. I understood, but rationalized that we were making money and eventually everything would fall into place.

I could go on and on with my brilliant hindsight, but I'm sure you're seeing the denial in this picture very clearly.

So here we are doing great business at Fishbones and good business at Roosters. We've got *twice* the amount of employees and problems. We're not making twice the amount of money, but we're spending twice the amount. Our having more was not more at all. Instead, the reality of our having more was that we were sinking and had a lot less. We were also making messes out of ourselves and killing the success we had.

The *big mistake* was my letting Dylan spend that much borrowed money on opening a simple space. For half the amount, we could have bought another prime, existing business location on the Upper Upper West Side.

Dumber got dumbest when we allowed Mr. X to take advantage of our lack of business and borrowing skills. Here, again, we or more importantly, I, ate the big one by not heeding our accountant's advice and drawing the line in the sand with Mr. X. Instead we were financially overextended, over staffed and I was extremely over worked. So like many other businesses in this huge metropolis, we began to rob Peter to pay Paul and had to deal with some pretty silly, sad and pathetic management and employee situations.

What was gained at Roosters? Nothing, I think. We provided jobs, improved the landlord's property and paid handsome interest to Mr. X. For almost two years, we did all right, but I was beginning to listen more and more to the accountants and for the first time cut Mr. X's profit sharing from Fishbones to an amount that absorbed some of his interest points on the Roosters loan. I also negated and sent back to him the Roosters loan contracts that had Fishbones as collateral. Since he was a stockholder in Fishbones, he had to comply. The Roosters loan was restructured to the best of my ability.

I then became a more demanding overseer of both businesses and for a while it worked so well that I found an Upper East Side location for our third place, Mamacitia's Fajitas Grill. I also cut out all of our perks and let Dylan and Fred know their salaries were based on time put on the job, and that had to match mine.

Then I fired two of their managers. One was a drunken thief at Fishbones that I found one early morning passed out on the bar with our safe full of money at his feet. It must have taken him hours to pry the safe out of the office floor and another hour to carry it upstairs to the front door. Lucky for me he had also drunk himself into oblivion. After I woke him up with an ice cube shower and the police, he claimed he rescued our safe from "invaders of the night forces!"

The other was a cokehead sex acrobat that got all tied up one night at Roosters. Luckily, he somehow had gotten the office secured before his friends tied him to Jorge's prep table, and covered him with fruits, vegetables, honey, flour and a lot of whipped cream. I first found the manager because my partners had long commutes. When I saw him, I first opened the office to see that the safe contained our money. I then saw his Polaroid's and the camera. I took a picture of him on the prep table and then untied him and made him clean up the kitchen and leave.

I used these two incidents to force both Dylan and Fred into recognizing that if they didn't do more, it was over. We were on the ass end of the sleigh ride and serious cuts had to be made.

Fred fired a minority female for stealing a lot of money at Fishbones. She filed a $50,000 complaint at the Human Resources Department, claiming he had sexually fondled her and when she said no, he fired her. She got $5,000 of our money.

I fired a guy for being a sour puss and a negative brain drain as a waiter at Roosters and he filed a complaint at Human Resources. He claimed I fired him for being gay. I was shocked when I read these papers because I'd hired him because he was the boyfriend of one of our waitresses. This guy got $11,000 of ours. I'm sure they both got more from other employment situations but when it happens to you, it stir-fries your brain.

Two incidents in one evening did in Fred. One that really pissed me off was when Fred insulted and upset my friend who I mentioned in the beginning of the Fishbones story. Remember he had let me use his Mr. Chicken investment to secure the Fishbones lease? I always let him eat or drink for free whenever he wanted to because of his generosity. Without his generosity Fishbones never would've existed. He rarely took advantage of my offer. One night Fred called him a free loader in front of his friends in some attempt at being friendly/funny. To his credit, the guy called me from Fishbones and told me the story and I asked him to stay there with his friends and enjoy their meal. I'd be there shortly.

When I got there, I found Fred having drinks in our office with someone who wasn't his wife. In front of her, I told him to get his ass upstairs to apologize or he was leaving for good. He jumped up at me and I pushed him back into his seat and gave him some sharp words to live by. He of course started crying and tried to apologize and I told him to save his tears and start looking for something else to do because it was over between us.

Later that same evening he was stupidly talking to customers about the Mexican thieves that worked in our kitchen and how the menu needed changes. Pele asked me to get him out of the dining room and out of the restaurant. Pele said he'd buy Fred out of our deal if we would let him. I went and got Fred and took him behind the restaurant. Then I pointed out to him his shortcomings in this business. My style at this time in my life with all the different pressures I was under was not pretty, civil or free of physical acting out. After our confrontation, Dylan made Fred the night manager of Roosters every night of the week and told him if he didn't like it, he could leave with nothing.

In spite of further personal problems with all my partners, I thought a third place could pull us out of what I perceived as a personally threatening financial disaster. My fantasy or hope was that if we hit the number again, I could leave with a few bucks, a healthy track record and strike out on my own. While I was having these pipe dreams and working on the lease deal, Mr. X, Dylan, and Fred, who all felt I was being too overbearing, were circling my wagon.

Dum Dada Dum!

CHAPTER 13

Restaurant Divorce

13. Restaurant Divorce

No matter how I begin this last chapter, I always go back to being a youngster working in some capacity at my parent's place or my uncle John's where there were always problems. Irish business and household problems are different from Latin family problems and from Italian family problems, so you would think. One constant remains through all the different racial and cultural configurations in the food service industry: It is stressful, hard and very demanding work done day in and day out to feed a hungry planet.

I witnessed cruel behavior by different parents, relatives and employees in the various restaurants in which I worked. I'd be kept awake at night by the alcoholic craziness that my parents brought home. It scared me so much that whenever the popular TV show "Divorce Court" would appear in the afternoons on the kitchen TV in our restaurant, I would always try to distract my mother from watching the program out of the fear that it would encourage her to go get on the show.

Sadly, we all know about divorce from many personal experiences. A tennis partner of mine is a divorce attorney who hates his work. I once asked him why. He told me, "A divorce opens the door to the vile snake pit of human nature and emotions!" I never brought up the subject again.

It doesn't matter how it began, or what happened in the middle that led to the horrible finale. Restaurant divorce is a car crash end to shared hopes, sacrifices and money invested that went way wrong. This bitter ending to any effort that succeeds or fails is like having your flesh publicly peeled off your body and letting anybody you've ever known see the smoldering ashes of your tortured soul's dreams.

In setting up our restaurant, Paolo and I drew up the one page buy-sell agreement mentioned in Chapter 8. We signed it in our lawyer's office. It looked something like this:

> "In the event that the partners in the restaurant Tusculum decide to leave the business for any reason, each partner has the right to remain or leave for the following agreed price. The exiting partner receives his start up investment at prime-rate interest over a three-year time span. The exiting partner also shares in the profits at 15% of the net during the same three years. At the end of the three years and the complete satisfaction of the exiting partner's debt, his stock and all Tusculum properties and rights will be assigned to the remaining partner."

Though not completely painless, this simple document allows partners to disengage without much trouble. Then, before a split-up is a reality, each partner has signed and agreed to the buy-sell agreement and is familiar with how things would end. The craziness that can come out of protracted legal battles is eliminated and a settlement can be worked out and executed within days. Then both satisfied parties can pick up the pieces and go on with their lives.

I don't know how many times I've said in this book that one point or another is the most important but this is may be the biggest. To prove my point I ask you to read on.

My N.Y.C. Story Part 10

BACK TO THE WEIRD WORLD

The businesses and growth of any neighborhood in any part of any city can be stymied and affected by tragedy. If the media sensationalizes that tragedy, businesses of every type are devastated. Unfortunately for Roosters, a young actress fought for her life on the rooftop across the street from us and lost. Her screams for help were not heard or ignored. The crime angered the city and fear stopped all after-dark activity in the neighborhood.

The media would have run that story for at least a week, but on that Wednesday, Chicken Little fell out of the sky and onto Wall Street. Wall Street sunk 500 points and was running scared. The following week they were handing out pink slips and the S and L travesties of the Reagan years were showing up on our radar screens. The paper bond market that Wall Street built through the eighties that made many people rich was on fire and the heads of big players were about to roll as large firms went down. These two incidents so strongly affected the changing Roosters neighborhood that no matter what we did, we couldn't get people to come. Fishbones stalled a little and Mamacitia's did the same.

Fate didn't deal us a harsh blow. We did it to ourselves and I take most of the responsibility for that. I should have had my priorities and desires in check. I shouldn't have been afraid to either rid myself of my partners or sell to them and walk away in the very beginning. If I really had known and owned what I really wanted, I would never have found myself in this position. No matter what afflicts your life or businesses, if you're overextended when tragedy or calamity strikes, *the nightmare begins*. All your monthly expenses are still due, the interest meter on borrowed money continues to tick and taxes and liquor cycles are ignored. When the stealing from Peter to pay Paul maneuvers take over your way of doing business, the beginning of the end creeps into your consciousness and in your heart of hearts you know its over.

We closed down Roosters and made it into a weekend college club. The Country Club held its own and made some principle loan payments, but the interest was brutal. Fishbones came back stronger than ever, Mamacitia's was doing well and another year had passed by. I could never shake the feelings I had of making a change or staying and letting the debt bury us. I didn't have a crystal ball that predicted the recession. I just had this gut feeling that while everything was stable I wanted out. The time was right. My partners also saw it that way. Our accountants valued my buyout at $250,000—half to be paid up front and the other half to be paid out in 36 monthly payments. I signed myself off of any corporate debt responsibility and Mr. X and the two partners absorbed my stock.

The moment I left Fishbones with my checks to go to the bank, the locks and menus were being changed. Fred was overseeing painters who were changing murals and logo designs that Eric Brown and others had done at Fishbones. If the old cliché "if it ain't broke, don't fix it!" wasn't deadly correct in this situation, I'm ready for the glue factory. I lived on the same block as Fishbones and it was starting to look shabby. I saw little of the new owners and more of their new management staff.

Many of the people who worked for me left those three restaurants in due time after my departure and went on to successfully open and operate their own places in the City. The absentee ownership of Fishbones, Mamacitia's and the Country Club turned Mr. X into a nightmare for the partners, because since they were not there during the operating hours of business, weird things became commonplace. Mr. X was very intolerant of that type of stupidity and started to see things the way I had seen them the year before.

Eventually Jorge also left and I met him in Guatemala where he and his wife were vacationing with family and friends. I loved Guatemala and became inspired to do something different than I'd ever done before. I'd asked Jorge if he wanted to try something different with me in the future and he said he needed sometime to finish up with his classes at the culinary school, but would be ready in six months.

I spent a considerable amount of time in Guatemala and El Salvador, collecting many things and some understanding of the cultures. I began to understand where the great work ethic of these people came from and also learned what they suffered through trying to get to America. Politics are for others, but I'd only say if you get here like our forefathers you deserve a shot and my respect. All of us who travel know the pecking order of the world and the different components that make up our world. We also admire all those who try to change it by coming to this country willing to work hard, trying to make it.

I loved the fact that Jorge was committed to school and enjoying what he was learning. When he was almost done, he told me his wife was pregnant, but that he wanted to do what we had spoken about in Guatemala. I told him I was almost ready, but had a few ends to tidy up myself.

My most important concern was that my ex-partners were not paying me because they said the businesses were way off and the money wasn't there for me. But the money was there for them and their families through all their mismanagement. They continued not working evening shifts and tried managing the businesses over the phone. Mr. X watched them miss principle payments and the interest continued to compound.

I was furious that I was never going to see my money unless I wanted to use lawyers to get back on board the sinking ship. Negative on that! The $100,000 I lost was the cost of my MBA in the restaurant business. I had learned what I really wanted from these experiences. I now knew how to go about setting it up right from the beginning and I was ready. So I looked at the glass half-full, instead of half empty. I went about my business with complete confidence in what Jorge and I were setting out to do because we both shared strong feelings about what not to do.

14. P. S.—To Summarize

THE GYPSY WOLF CANTINA STORY

One night I had a dream in which I was a kid who had two dogs that could sing like parrots, but they would never sing around anyone else but me. One morning I took them to Church with me where I was the altar boy for early mass. I was planning to ask the priest, Father Austin, to bless them so they'd stop making a fool out of me with my friends. During the mass, they started singing in the room where I'd left them next to the altar. The look on the priest's face was like the one on the angel Clarence in the movie "It's a Wonderful Life," when he's talking to God. After a hurried mass, Father Austin followed me to the dogs that were still singing and he blessed them over and over again, saying they were Gypsy Wolves because they could sing in Latin. I never forgot that name. It doesn't matter where a good name, great ideas, or divine inspiration come from as long as you remember them.

 I was soon learning all about wolves and I started collecting everything and anything that had to do with them. I was amazed at the impact wolves have had on mankind. I loved their independence, family structure and, of course, their singing. From another trip to Guatemala, I brought back over a hundred carved Wolf masks for the walls of The Gypsy Wolf Cantina that was coming together in my mind's eye.

 Jorge and I began taking drives up and down both sides of the Hudson River looking at different locations advertised for sale in the New York Times. We'd also stop in at real estate offices in the towns that interested us. The drives were very enjoyable for many reasons, but the main reason was that we wanted to live and work in the countryside we were discovering and learning about. Our on-going search for the right situation in the country seemed like a natural progression to what we had done for many years in the city.

On one of those drives I heard a woman being interviewed on the radio tell the interviewer that she was living "The New American Dream." She said in a cautionary way that she was able to live and make a living in the country. That little comment made Jorge and I get more focused on talking about what we each really wanted. We each wanted a restaurant outside of the city and lives that were very different from the ones we were living.

That fall we criss-crossed the Hudson Valley and thought we were back in Central America. The beauty of the Hudson Valley is beyond my descriptive abilities except to say that great American artists of the Hudson Valley School painted it. Wealthy American Industrialists and Presidents built their estates on the riverbanks, as did religious and educational institutions. They all joined the people who centuries ago had settled and worked on the river and in its valleys. From generation to generation, they stayed because they never wanted to live anywhere else. 'Cause if you're leaving the river, where could you be goin'? This area is the real Disneyland, I once heard a local say.

We were getting pretty discouraged by the middle of winter. One day after driving all around areas surrounding Albany, we found ourselves driving through Woodstock on our way back to the city. It was a bone chilling, dark damp day and hardly anyone was out except people shopping at the supermarket and local video store. The center of town was empty except for the various shop owners shoveling snow and salting icy sidewalks. Driving was very difficult for Jorge on the sanded icy roads and I said: "Let's head back whenever you can turn around."

Eventually, a couple of miles out of town, we pulled into a large empty parking lot with a boarded up building set back in the center of the property with For Sale, For Lease and For Rent signs all over the building. We drove over to the building with the gravel crunching under our tires, a sound I love but hadn't heard in years.

We got out of the car and walked around the property and building until we could pull back some plywood and peek in through a window. The place was trashed and broken pipes from the freezing weather had flooded the floors. The spraying waters were creating a huge sapphire blue ice sculpture. I have no idea how that ice got backlit, but I'd never seen ice like that before. There was a small bar and about fifteen tables in the place. In one corner was a big potbelly stove, a jukebox and, along the far wall, a shuffleboard table. Behind the tavern was an Olympic-size, collapsed pool with burned out pool houses on one side of the property and the remains of a miniature golf course on the other side.

We figured the tavern was where pool guests and golfers hung out and ate in the old days when insurance costs didn't kill those types of businesses. The size of the parking lot told us that someone did a serious seasonal business in the old days. The razed remains of what was left was beyond repair, but when we got our frozen bodies back into the car and looked at the boarded up little restaurant, we both knew it was perfect for our Gypsy Wolf Cantina concept. While we were sitting there I could visualize what it was going to look like with a full parking lot. Jorge commented on the amount of passing traffic as I wrote down the phone number.

We started back down the road to Woodstock. This time as we slowly drove through the small town, we took down the phone numbers of three other places in the restaurant graveyard. I thought to myself that Woodstock would love what we would be bringing to their town, but they had to be a critical audience if four restaurants were for rent in a town of 7000 people. Yet we were so wired with excitement on the drive home that we pulled over and had a bite to eat at a Mexican restaurant in Spring Valley and I called the phone number of the icy pool restaurant.

I spoke to the owner and told him about the leaking pipes. I also asked him his asking price for the sale of the property and for the monthly rent. After he gave me some shocking numbers, I told him I wanted to see the inside of the building tomorrow, if possible, because I would be in the area looking at another place. He said great and we set a time to meet. He told me he was going right down to the restaurant to repair the plumbing leaks because he also had someone else looking at the restaurant tomorrow. The guy was talking like the big frog in the little pond, starting with his $300,000 selling price, the $2,500 monthly rent plus a fixture fee and his other interested party wanting to also see the place tomorrow.

But that was O.K. I found out the place had been empty for almost two years and I'm sure if we really liked it enough, we could make the ideal deal with this guy. He wanted a tenant and what he had purposefully overvalued could be negotiated down in different ways after we'd seen what was in the place.

That night I spoke at length with a long time Woodstock resident and learned a lot about that community. I mainly learned that the area boomed during the late seventies and early eighties just like everywhere during Reaganomics. After the 1987 crash and recession, the area had a big economic correction like everywhere else. And when IBM started downsizing its Hudson Valley operations, businesses suffered and closed. He told me that the spot I was interested in was the greatest in the seventies and that since then the restaurant had been turned over so many times he couldn't remember the name of the last effort, other than to tell me it was a scary, out of control bar. He agreed with me that the location was one of the best in the area. He also thought we'd do well because our concept would appeal to the locals, unlike the other closed places in town. I got a lot more out of our conversation and afterwards thanked him with the promise of an invite to the rehearsal dinner.

While Jorge and I drove back up early the next day, we discussed our strategy for our meeting with the landlord. Basically, what we wanted to know was the condition of the mechanical parts of the place. We needed to check out the condition of the plumbing, electric, septic, roof, and hood systems. We assumed the kitchen and dining area furniture and equipment would have no value or use. What really mattered was the structural integrity of the building. After we found out what had to be done to the mechanical elements, we would measure the entire space and make some calculations. With this information we could tell the guy what we wanted to do within an hour.

The meeting went very well. Once Jorge and I had all the information we needed, we told the landlord that we were going for coffee; we'd get him one, and that we'd be right back. I told Jorge that I felt I could transform that tired and beat up space into something special for us, but the amount of work it would take would really challenge us. Jorge agreed that the work wouldn't bother us, if we made the right deal. Based on what we saw that morning, I guesstimated we could be open for business at some point during the coming summer at a cost somewhere in the area of $50,000-60,000. We figured out our offer right then and there in the diner:

1. We wanted a ten-year lease starting at $1250 a month.
2. His fixture fee of $10,000 was absurd since all the equipment in the place was garbage. We'd give him $5,000 at a hundred a week. We looked at that amount as a cost of doing business and a gesture that would get us the deal we wanted.
3. We would give him a $2,000 deposit as first and last month's rent. We wanted three months free rent, and after those three months the rent would be $750 a month until we opened.
4. We would also tell him we only wanted a two or three page straight forward lease and if he was going to be named as the sole insured he could pay his half of the fire insurance just like we'd pay our share of any tax increase.
5. We would pay $1500 a year fixed through out the length of the lease for the total property behind the restaurant and wanted the right to sublease it if we so desired.
6. We wanted right of first refusal in the event that he had an opportunity to sell the property.

We got him a coffee and Danish and went back to the restaurant. I told him our offer and he protested. I stopped him and said, "I know the history of your problems with this restaurant and I know Jorge and I could make a go of it here, but without a cooperating landlord we'll have to look elsewhere."

He tried to convince us that he had a better deal with someone else and I said, "That's the best we can do. I don't think you're going to find better qualified people than Jorge and I for long term tenants."

He thought on that for a full minute and then stood up and shook our hands and said, "Gentlemen you got a deal. A damn good deal. Let's go over to my attorney's office so I can get some of your money today!"

We followed him to the nearby city of Kingston to his lawyer's office. His lawyer was very nice and happy to do as we wished to satisfy his client, our new landlord. In fact, the guy was so helpful and forthright; we hired him to be our attorney. We left his office with a signed lease, a local insurance agent's name who handled most restaurant needs, the name of an attorney who could help us secure a liquor license and incorporation, and a realistic idea of what lay ahead for our venture in the township of Woodstock from our new attorney who had been a Woodstocker for some thirty years.

We opened a business checking account at a bank in Woodstock and then we went to meet the town's building inspector. He couldn't have been nicer or more informative. No, he told us, we won't need a building permit unless we're making structural changes, but we will need to purchase a sign permit. He also suggested that we have the landlord fill in the empty pool even though it was fenced in. Most important, he told us that if we did not open for business within the next forty three days, the parcel would loose its grandfathered zoning variance as a restaurant serving alcohol, because no business had been conducted there for almost two years. The parcel would revert back to Commercial Light Industrial usage only.

We immediately got back to our new attorney and had him write a letter to the building inspector's office informing them that we would be open for a pancake breakfast on the last Sunday of the current month.

If you don't go to the local building inspector right away to check out all these different local zoning rules and regulations, your plans can definitely be sucker-punched. That afternoon, we picked up a local phone book and looked for the nearest Mexican food restaurants. There were two. We went to the closest for lunch and for a look at our competition. Lunch was very disappointing, to say the least, and the place was fifteen miles from Woodstock and not in our competitive territory.

After lunch, we met with the insurance agent and took out a general liability and fire policy to cover us until we opened for business. Then we met with our liquor license attorney. We filled out incorporation papers, evenly split the stock, drew up a one-page Buy-Sell agreement between us, and filed for our liquor license. We asked the attorney to recommend an accountant. Without blinking an eye, he said all the better restaurants worked with Jacob Halpern, as did his firm.

We went to see the accountant and he lived up to his top billing. He was terrific; he had us comfortable with his way of doing our business immediately. We set up our bookkeeping the way he needed it done so Theresa, his assistant, could take all our start up costs and expenses off of our Quicken report and log them into their Data System. Every dime spent was to be paid out of our business account by check. Jay also had us pay out of that account five hundred dollars a week into our payroll account. We each drew $250 a week as a pay check that his office issued not so much for the money but mainly to get ourselves user friendly with their payroll service and to have a little cash in our pockets for living expenses. We also signed power of attorney papers with Jay, so his office could issue and sign checks out of our payroll account for all the different State and Federal tax bills. His office would also prepare our employee W2 forms at the end of the year, as well as Jorge's and my taxes. The cost of his services was very fair and the value of his services to me, were over the top. I happen to be a person who can make a dollar in this business, but I'm not very good at bookkeeping. I was so relieved after seeing that Jorge and Theresa were connected on what had to be done each week with the bookkeeping. Our new relationship with Jay's office now freed me to get to the task ahead: transforming our leased space into the Gypsy Wolf Cantina, within budget with a target opening date during the summer months.

I went into the new project with great energy and confidence in what we were about to create. I knew what I wanted and I knew how to go about it. Our new venture was set up by Jorge and I to be trouble-free and on our terms. We knew we could provide the Product in a fun place at the right price. Our target audience wasn't seasonal tourists or second homeowners. We wanted a place that served and valued the locals. If they supported our effort, the rest would fall in line.

I came up with a one liner that we've stayed with since day one. "The Gypsy Wolf Cantina is a place where you can take a healthy bite out of your appetite, not your wallet." We created our menu based on that idea. The important point is that after all I've done in this business, I'm now doing it the way it should be done! There *is* life after death in the restaurant business, but only if you get it right from the beginning.

We took critical measurements of the building and a lot of pictures so we could work on what we wanted to change while we still lived in the city. We then put pen to paper and, as you can see on the following pages, we reworked the space as we got it into a design that served our concept.

We then worked on our business plan and budget. Soon enough, we rented a farmhouse from some wonderful people who are still great friends of ours. They were long time residents of the area and knew everything about everyone and what the area needed in the food business. After they ate our food with us in the farmhouse and knew what we were up to; they spread the word.

We began working on the place in the middle of a freezing March. Even with the heat on from a basement boiler and a forced air heater, the place was frigid because none of the windows were thermal-pane and the building was poorly insulated. I knew if these problems were not fixed now, no one would want to eat here next winter. The first thing we did was go up into the attic crawl space and put back together the forced air furnace duct system. It was a dirty job and took a few days, but at least the hot air was now going into the dining room and not out the roof. We did the same thing with the basement duct system. The result was more heat in the building. I put in three overhead fans and set them so they forced the rising hot air back down from the ceilings. We then caulked leaks around the windows and everywhere that we had cold air coming through the walls I pulled the wall boards off and stuffed insulation behind them. By the end of the week and at minimal expense, we had the place comfortably warm so we could begin working.

After our first few weeks in Woodstock in the dead of winter, I got a pretty good idea of the economic dynamics of the town. The health food store did serious business in the town shopping center and was rivaled only by the video store for daylong customer traffic. But the busiest and sharpest hands-on business owners in town were Vinny at his meat market and Andre at his lumberyard. I became friendly with these two owner-operators by doing business with them everyday. Vinny and Andre were guys I could easily relate and listen to. They both grew up here and had seen almost everything imaginable come and go through this town as they worked and succeeded here. Basically, they both enjoyed who they were and loved their work. They also both had tremendous work ethics and pulled the train in their stores. I love these guys today and have great fun with them because they supported and appreciated what Jorge and I did. They are good friends and customers who, out of mutual respect, send a lot of people our way. They are also the barometers of this small town's business activity. They've seen different boom and bust cycles over the years and they've prospered through the good and bad times because they consistently provide personal service and quality products. They do it on their own terms and are intolerant of any nonsense that interferes with their standards. I learned a lot from each of these men about conducting business in this town and I'm thanking them here for that.

I got permission from the landlord to put all of the equipment from our leased space into the pavilion behind the restaurant. We got some help and emptied the building of everything we would never use or want. Two dumpster loads later we had the place cleaned out and ready for our improvements. On the following page is the space as it was, followed by a drawing of the empty space; last is the re-worked floor plan for The Gypsy Wolf Cantina.

Old Restaurant Floor Plan

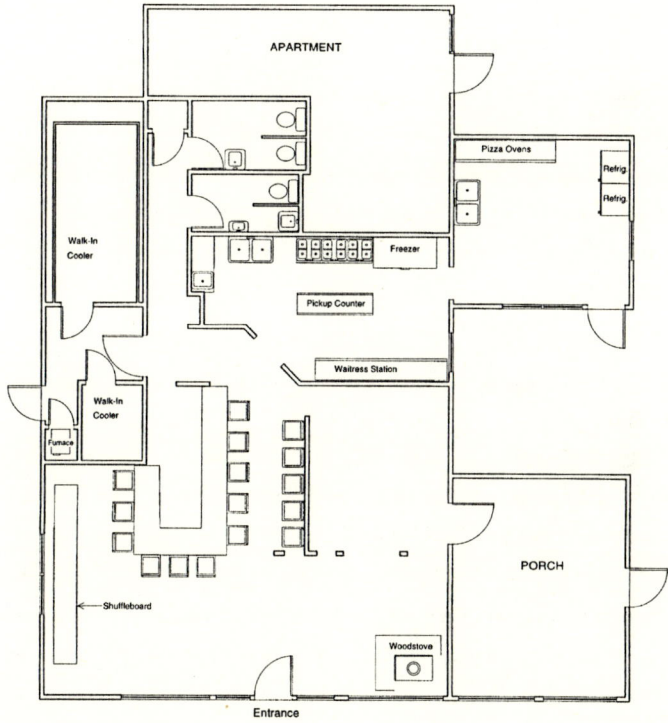

Old Restaurant Floor Plan:

Much renovation was necessary in the front of the restaurant. The woodstove, and shuffleboard had to go. Also, the porch was rotted and needed rebuilding.

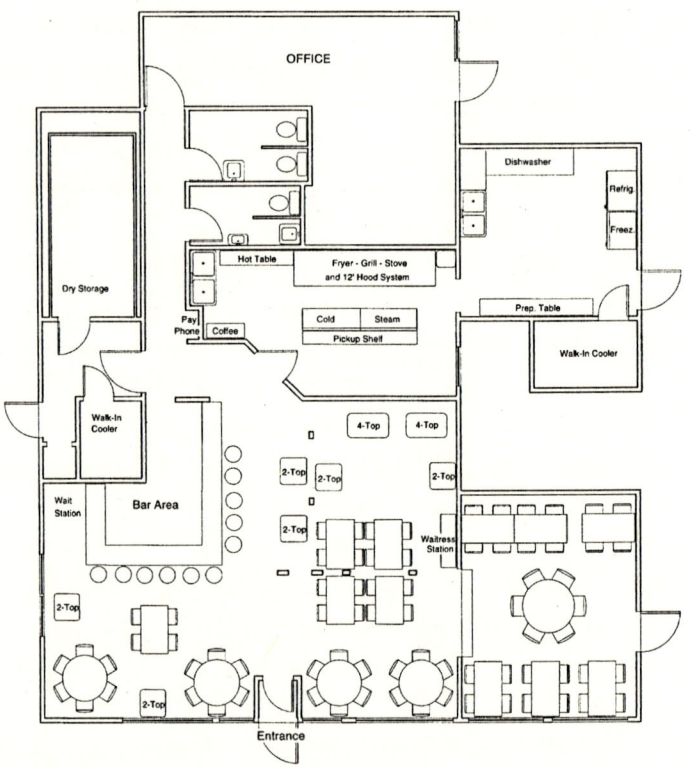

Gypsy Wolf Cantina Restaurant Floor Plan:
We made several improvements to the original restaurant:

- We enlarged and improved the septic drainage field, and installed a grease trap ahead of the septic tank.

- We installed a new gas boiler in the basement and put baseboard heat all around the building.
- The bar was enlarged and we moved the existing wall to provide more passage space.
- We added a windbreak entrance and reversed the opening of the front door.
- We installed thermal windows throughout the building (this is the Catskills).
- We enclosed the porch and made a year-round dining area.
- We added a walk-in cooler near to the preparation table and created a dishwashing area in the same back area.
- The apartment became our office.

The kitchen is almost exactly like the one Jorge had at Fishbones. Small, efficient and laid out for easy in and out traffic. The prep room is a comfortable size with lots of shelving for the dishwasher. In the future, I plan to put a walk-in cooler outside near the prep room. I then can use the walk in behind the bar for beer only. If business warrants it, I can shrink that walk in and expand the bar area.

In the dining area, I took down the existing wall near the bar and made room for wait-staff traffic and side-to-side two-tops. I replaced the walls and columns with old, salvaged six-inch by six-inch timbers. I also covered the sloping drywall ceilings with old beat up sheet metal roofing materials. Pieces from the set of the play, Talley's Folly, became the connecting railings joining the posts and dividing the whole space into nice separate cozy dining areas that would accommodate old wood booths that I salvaged from different sources. I also pulled drywall off the walls in the dining area and machine sanded the wood I found underneath.

Soon, the place was dramatically transformed and I felt real good about how it would work. We had pulled up and thrown away tons of beer-soaked layers of carpeting and rented floor sanders to somehow give new life to the barn timber floor that had been blackened over the years by neglect and water. We sanded that floor with coarse industrial grit paper for a week until we got a lighter and cleaner floor. The space just came alive with the lighter flooring but I thought we should bleach the floor, so when we applied the polyurethane finish coats, it wouldn't darken too much and disappear. We got ten coats of polyurethane on the floor and stayed off it for a month while it hardened.

We took Jorge's kitchen equipment list to our friend Mickey Moscovitz at Daroma Restaurant Supply on the Bowery in Manhattan. Over the years Mickey has handled all our equipment needs. His prices and personal attention work very well for me when I'm spending serious money on a new venture. He understands what's at risk in this business and like any good salesman he knows that if I'm satisfied with his service and product, I'll be a long time customer. That attitude carries over to any problems with anything purchased from Daroma. If an item he sells you doesn't work or satisfy you, he wants you to bring it back for full credit and he'll get you what you need. He promptly takes care of his customer's needs. He recently told me that business was better than ever and he couldn't remember a time when so many new people without a clue as to how to run a restaurant were spending a lot of money on the Bowery. He also said they'll show up again in the restaurant obituary in the New York Times Auction Page, which is why he won't ever sell restaurant equipment to any living relatives or close friends—but they're always asking him.

"Never!" he roars with a laugh. "Never ever!"

I rest my case.

We spent close to $5,000 at Daroma for a new Wolf range, a salamander-cheese melter, a double-door, used refrigeration unit, a gas steam table, a food processor, an industrial blender and a worktable. We spent another $3,000 at other Bowery businesses for plates, glasses, silverware, kitchen items and some used tables and chairs.

Through the regional Want-Ad Digest we found some great bargains: a 36-inch Magic Chef grill used for six months for $1,000; a Jackson corner-feed dishwasher with sinks and drain counters for $900; a brand new Taylor Margarita machine used only for a summer business for $2200; and a large Bain Marie with compressor for $150. Shelving, booths and assorted other restaurant furniture were found in nearby used restaurant supply places for about another $1,000.

So by pickin', diggin' and dickerin' we had the equipment, furniture and tools we needed to open for a total of $13,250. At the end of the first month we had spent the following:

1. Lease expenses — $6500
2. Liquor license fee — $6000
3. Insurance costs — $2000
4. Legal expenses — $2000
5. Accounting costs — $1000
6. Relocating expenses — $4000
7. Salary draw — $1000
8. Utility deposit — $1000
9. Equipment — $14000
10. Miscellaneous — $2000

Month ending total — $40,500

We're tight with a buck and do almost everything ourselves, but within thirty days we'd spent almost two thirds of our budget. The good news is that we were all paid up in the rent department and had only inventory for the restaurant as the last big expense. The bad news was that the State Liquor Authority was downsizing and consolidating all of its regional offices into two branches, Albany and Manhattan. Anyone applying during this time could expect a longer wait. How long? No one seemed to know and that bothered me a lot.

Spring came and went and the rented space was now looking very much the way I wanted it. Eric Brown did a lot of fun paintings, signs and logo work with my ideas and the interior of the restaurant now felt and looked like a place where you could really relax and enjoy yourself. It was and is very cool.

We reinforced the kitchen floor. Jorge re-plumbed all the kitchen plumbing. I did the needed electrical changes. We installed all the equipment, had the Ansel System activated and all the refrigeration tuned up. We were now ready to start taste testing the food and finalizing the menu. Everyday Jorge created and cooked different dishes. We would eat and discuss what worked and what didn't. Soon enough we had our menu in place and felt that our food would appeal to our customer base. Half of our menu was vegetarian and our entire menu was fresh and wholesome foods made from scratch.

We priced out the menu based on food costs of 30% for our projected sales volume. The menu was priced quite affordably and our customers would certainly get quality meals and value for their dollar.

Summer came in all its glory and we started cleaning up the property around the restaurant. It occurred to me that if I lit the outside of the restaurant with thousands of lights the place would look like it was floating in the parking lot after dark. I wanted to paint the outside of the restaurant a lively color, something very different from the existing barn red. But first I wanted to cover the existing, newly shingled roof with metal roofing. After we put on the new roof, I started priming the exterior of the building for a light turquoise color. Working outside we met a lot of different people, some wanting jobs, some curious and some just plain nosy.

On the day I started spraying the turquoise on the building, I had some friends visiting from the city with their newborn daughter. They were both very experienced New York City restaurant people who were thinking about relocating up this way and the work we had done really excited them. I thought to myself, if these people moved up here and worked with us at the Cantina, the heart of our staff would be in place. During a break from painting we were all standing and looking at the color when some jerks driving by in a pickup truck threw a beer can at me and yelled, "Get out of Woodstock!" Needless to say, that really upset us, and my friends left, never to return.

I told different people what had happened. The consensus was that there was some weirdness connected to the prior life of our new space and a certain element of that fringe would test me because I was just another city person coming here to take something away from them. I began to understand the great divide between the locals and upwardly mobile, second homeowners in this area. A lot of locals were being forced into hardship by property and school taxes that, for many generations, were manageable, but now, because of excessive assessment, were unmanageable and unfair. A lot of fine folks had to give up land that they loved in order to survive. I don't know the answers to these problems; I only want to succeed and to be judged by that. Plus, I'm not going to be intimidated by anyone.

Our plan was to only be open four hours a night from 5-9 p.m. weeknights and 5-10 p.m. on the weekends. We would be a family place where obnoxious behavior and drunkenness would not be tolerated. "Be nice or be gone" were and still are the terms by which we conduct business at our restaurant. Telling people no, or telling people to leave didn't bother me if it was necessary, but realizing that if some idiot is not stopped or confronted, it could affect our business, did bother me. So we let everyone who we hired know exactly our policy on liquor sales and unacceptable customer behavior.

When I finished painting the building, I put up some garage sale shutters. The change was dramatic. The tin roof, the turquoise paint and new shutters had transformed the building into our cherished Cantina. I then put a thousand colored lights on the outside of the building. On a warm July evening, I turned them on when it got dark and the parking lot started filling up. It just happened spontaneously, so we invited the people in for a look at the restaurant. Jorge and I put up some free samples and the visitors responded with compliments and good luck wishes. We turned off the lights after the last visitor left and headed home very concerned about the fading summer and still no liquor license.

By now we had used up our free rent time and, pretty much, used up our budget of $60,000, except for $5000 put aside for opening inventory and training expenses. We quit paying ourselves. I sold my car for $5500 and bought a truck for $1200. I felt that the interior decoration could use more to really send it over the top, so I got a cheap ticket back to Guatemala and returned within a week with what I needed, spending a total of $1500. The remaining money got us through some long days, until, mercifully, we got the call from our liquor attorney.

The following week we were interviewed at the State Liquor Authority and left Albany with our license. On the way back to Woodstock we made the decision to open in ten days during mid-week in a low-key way, so that by the weekend everyone would be more comfortable and secure if we got busy.

Back in town, we pulled into the supermarket parking lot. Out of the corner of my eye across the street at the gas station, I saw the pickup truck and the guy that threw the beer can at me and scared my friends. I told Jorge to go shopping and I'd be right back.

I had no idea what I was going to do as I crossed the street with my heart beating like a drum. The truck's driver finished putting gas in the truck and went inside to pay. The guy that threw the beer can was sitting and smoking in the passenger seat. I got in on the driver's side and introduced myself. I explained who I was, what I was doing and what I thought of him throwing the beer can. He said nothing. As the driver returned, I left the truck feeling a lot better. I loved where I now lived and what we created at the Cantina. It was going to bring a lot of enjoyment to many others and us and, no matter what, I was going to stand up for that effort.

We then put together our staff. Some of our extended family from New York moved up here with us and we had enough people in place to open. I now knew enough about our customer base that I didn't want to open until we were well rehearsed. I felt very strongly that we had a great looking place with a terrific menu, but the service had to be a serious professional statement so that the total experience gave our customers that *good feeling!*

We rehearsed everyday, and tasted all the foods and drinks. The night before our planned opening, Jorge's son was born. We opened the following week without a dollar spent on advertising and no phone number except for a public telephone. But it all worked out very well.

People came and they enjoyed our production, product and prices. Most significantly, the locals came, which was very satisfying because after the leaves fall, our town's population shrinks by more than half during weeknights. So when winter arrived and the plows were on the roads it was great to see the locals rolling into the parking lot happy to see us open like we'd been here forever.

The people of Woodstock warmly received us. They had no problems with our hours, our cash-only policy and the fact that we had no phone. I even brought the bar stools up out of the basement by the end of the first week and when I did encounter some of the good old boys wanting shots and Buttwipers, I'd just recite the Mexican beer list for them and say we didn't serve Budweiser. Some would stay, most would leave.

I had very few problems with anyone and felt that my no-nonsense way of running a restaurant came across very clearly. A DWI in New York State can really mess up your life, and cost you a fortune in legal fees and insurance. Thankfully, people get the message. Because of that, their drinking habits are very different in the nineties for the restaurant business. I had no problems with anyone. You could have knocked me over with a feather when one night, sitting at the bar with his wife and kid, was the guy who threw the beer can at me. I walked towards them and nodded hello and he asked for three cokes. When I turned to go get the cokes he said: "Please Mr. Gas Man." That got me laughing so hard I had to bite the inside of my mouth to stop. Seven years later, I'm still Mr. Gas Man and he and his family and friends are good customers.

Another night at the Cantina when I did get knocked over by a feather was when I met my wife Mariann.

So, hey, if you ever find yourself in this part of the world, drop by, because we'd be happy to see you. We received a nice review and I've put a copy of it and our menu for you in the pages that follow.

In parting, I'd like to refer you to some other fine restaurants in our community. Woodstock has some great restaurants with long track records that are owner-operated like the Gypsy Wolf Cantina. When you're in town, check out The Bear Café, The Landau Grill, the Blue Mountain Bistro and New World Home Cooking for more tasty meals.

Gypsy Wolf Cantina Review

Howlingly good

Bearsville's Gypsy Wolf Cantina leads the pack

By MARY DEIRDRE DONOVAN

AFTER the reviews that have run the last few times, I'm sure there must be some of you who wonder if I actually like anything. Well, I do. And this is a review about a place I liked a whole lot.

A friend at work told me about the Gypsy Wolf Cantina. I tried unsuccessfully to get the number from information. The mystery was cleared up when I spoke with William Durkin, one of the owners, who told us the restaurant wasn't quite geared up to handle large reservations, and so rather than have to turn people down, they simply decided to wait to install a phone. An interesting concept.

As you enter the restaurant (the exterior is a brilliant turquoise and impossible to miss as you drive out of Woodstock on the way to Bearsville) you are confronted with a huge wall filled with painted masks from Guatamala. There are curious, amusing, and beautiful illustrations of wolves throughout, and a huge poster of a yellow dinosaur with the inscription "Travel with humility." This appears to be something of a mantra for the owners and staff. Our waitress couldn't have been more delightful, and she even conferred a genuinely affectionate hug on the member of our little group who was celebrating a birthday.

But what I really want to tell you about are the margaritas and our meal. The luscious beverage is a mere $3, and to my taste, the best I've had in the entire Hudson Valley. They are made with a non-alcoholic Triple Sec, so they don't have that sickening sweet aftershock. These are not exactly like other margaritas, and if you like them sweet, you may be in for a surprise. The frozen margarita has an entirely different flavor from the "on the rocks" version, and both were good.

I began with a Mama-Lita's Black Bean Magic Soup; it is other-

CHECK, PLEASE

GYPSY WOLF CANTINA
★★★★
Where: Route 212, Bearsville
Price range: Dinner for two with a margarita or beer, including tax and tip, approximately $40
Hours: Open for dinner from 5 p.m., seven days a week
Handicap accessible: Yes
Reservations: Not possible
Credit cards: None
What the stars mean:
★ Fair
★★ Good
★★★ Very good
★★★★ Excellent
The stars are not meant to be used as a way to compare this restaurant to others. Each establishment is judged independently. Opinions are strictly those of the reviewer, and readers are urged to try the food for themselves.

worldly. The soup was creamy and smooth, and wonderfully light. The taste was fresh, pure, and distinctly earthy, the way beans actually do taste. It is served on a bed of rice with some appropriate and simple garnishes like radishes, scallions and sour cream that really did enhance the dish, not hide it. An interesting addition I've never had elsewhere was corn masitas (a little "dumpling" of cornmeal dough).

The vegetarian quesadilla boasts some out-of-the-ordinary ingredients such as jicama and red cabbage. The garnishes include radishes, scallions, jalapenos and guacamole yogurt. It was a hot, tasty appetizer. I had decided to have it as an entree after the soup, and I'm glad that I did. That made it easier for me to sample (heavily) the other entree platters at the table: the Gypsy Wolf platter and the Gypsy's Soul Kabobs.

The wolf platter is a monster of a meal. It contains grilled steak, chicken and shrimp, with various garnishes, rice, black beans and soft, warm flour tortillas. The tortillas here are handmade and measurably better than "store bought." This style of cooking is time-consuming, but when it is done with care, it is (as the menu proclaims) "fresh, wholesome nutritional, and free of preservative ... Buen Provecho."

The kabobs we tried were seafood and vegetables on a bed of rice and black beans. This is fine fresh food that is handled with care and respect. The chef and co-owner, Jorge Perez, is a man who understands balance. There were superb flavors in every portion of the meal, but none were drowned by any other, nor were chilis and hot salsas indiscriminantly splashed about.

I look forward to returning again and again to sample other offerings from the menu — salads with grilled chicken and fresh lettuces and vegetables with orange honey dressing, or enchiladas and burritos with Puebla red sauce, tostadas, and the big winner in the wonderful name category, Many Moons and Stars Soft Tacos.

Gypsy Wolf Menu, page 1 of 3

STARTERS

GUACAMOLE
A blend of fresh mashed avocados, tomatoes, onions, cilantro, fresh salsa, lemon juice and spices. Served in a bird nest flour tortilla shell.
$ 6.50

NACHOS
Mixture of blue and yellow corn chips topped with black beans, chipotle chile sauce, melted cheese, scallions and jalapeños.
$ 7.50

SUPER NACHOS
Blue and yellow corn chips covered with black beans, chipotle chile sauce, melted cheese, choice of grilled chicken or steak, topped with guacamole, sour cream, scallions, black olives and jalapeños.
$ 10.50 Made with shrimp $11.50

THE SANCHEZ FARM QUESADILLAS
A spinach tortilla filled with a mix of black beans, sautéed mushrooms, yellow squash, potato, zucchini and cheese. Served with a mixture of carrot, jicama, scallions, radishes and guacamole.
$ 9.95

VEGETARIAN QUESADILLAS
A flour tortilla folded and filled with cheese, sautéed vegetables and salsa cruda. served with a mixture of lettuce, carrots, jicama, scallions, radishes, yogurt guacamole and jalapeños.
$ 7.95 Made with a spinach tortilla add $1.00

CHICKEN QUESADILLAS
Flour tortilla filled with cheese, grilled chicken and chipotle chile sauce. Served with lettuce, scallions, guacamole, sour cream and jalapeños.
$ 8.95 Made with spinach tortilla add $1.00

SHRIMP QUESADILLAS
A flour tortilla stuffed with cheese, sautéed shrimps in a garlic chipotle sauce, vegetables, and served with small salad, guacamole, sour cream, and jalapeños.
$ 9.95

MAMA LITA'S BLACK BEAN MAGIC SOUP
Puree black beans, whole black beans, rice on bottom, corn masitas (corn dough), scallions, radishes, avocado, cheese and sour cream.
$ 4.95

PLATOS PARA LOS NIÑOS
A smaller serving of our enchilada, burrito and chimichanga  served with beans, rice and vegetables. $7.50  or grilled chicken with rice, beans and tortillas $8.50

EXTRA EXTRAS- WHEN THINGS ARE CHANGED, OR EXTRAS ADDED WE WILL CHARGE ACCORDINGLY. WITH PARTIES OF SIX OR MORE A 20% GRATUITY WILL BE ADDED. MASTERCARD AND VISA ACCEPTED.

Gypsy Wolf Menu, page 2 of 3

ENTREES

Each entree is a completely balanced meal made with a variety of fillings; Chicken, Cheese, Machaca (beef), or Sautéed vegetables. All foods are made daily from scratch and are served with rice, beans and sautéed vegetables. All entrees with stars can be made vegetarian.

THE FARMER'S MARKET SALAD WITH GRILLED CHICKEN.
A flour shell filled with a variety of the freshest garden vegetables we could find, blue corn chips, cheese or tofu, topped with slices of grilled chicken and your choice of dressing: creamy avocado or orange honey.
$ 10.50

#1 * ENCHILADAS OF THIS VALLEY *
Three corn tortillas wrapped around your choice of filling and topped with Puebla red sauce, melted cheese and black olives.
$ 10.50

#2 * THE HELP ME TO LIVE LONGER BURRITO *
A large flour tortilla filled with your choice of filling, beans and cheese. Topped with salsa and melted cheese.
$ 10.50

#3 *SPIRIT OF THIS VALLEY VEGETARIAN BURRITO *
A large flour tortilla filled with spinach, broccoli, watercress, mushrooms, tofu, and black beans. Topped with cheese and chipotle sauce.
$ 10.50 Made with spinach tortilla add $1.00

#4 * TOSTADAS WITHOUT BORDERS *
Three open crisp tortillas: one corn, one flour, one blue corn. Each topped with beans, your choice of filling, lettuce, salsa cruda, cheese, guacamole and black olives.
$ 10.50

#5 * THE HOLY DAY CHIMICHANGAS *
Two flour tortillas filled with your choice, beans, cheese and lightly fried. Topped with salsa cruda, sour cream and guacamole.
$ 10.50

COMBINATIONS FROM MAMACITA'S KITCHEN

#6 HER MONDAY NIGHT COMBO
A cheese enchilada with puebla red sauce, a small beef burrito and a chicken tostada.
$ 10.50

#7* MAMACITA'S FAVORITE VEGETARIAN COMBO *
A cheese enchilada with green tomatillo sauce, a small vegetable burrito and a guacamole tostada.
$ 10.50

#8 MY FAVORITE COMBO
A chicken enchilada with puebla red sauce, beef soft taco and a cheese enchilada with green tomatillo sauce.
$ 10.50

PELIGROSO!--DANGER! TO ALL OF YOU RESPONSIBLE FOR CHILDREN WE ASK YOU TO KEEP THEM CLOSE BY FOR THE OBVIOUS REASONS-SIZZLING PLATES-OUR BUSY WAIT STAFF AND THE COMFORT OF ALL OUR CUSTOMERS. THANK YOU.

Gypsy Wolf Menu, page 3 of 3

SPECIALS OF THE GYPSY WOLF

 # 9   *** THE SUPREME MASTER RULER'S ***
ENCHILADAS VERDES
Three handmade corn tortillas filled with grilled chicken or grilled steak,
onions, green chiles, sour cream, and green tomatillo sauce.
Served with vegetables, white rice and black beans.
$ 14.95

 # 10   **OUR GYPSY WOLF PLATTER.**
Grilled steak, grilled chicken, 3 grilled shrimps, guacamole, sour cream,
radishes, black olives, cheese, tomatoes, cilantro, lettuce, mixture of
carrots and jicama, rice, black beans and flour tortillas.
$ 14.95

 # 11   *** CORAZON Y PISTOLAS SIZZLING FAJITAS ***
Your choice of grilled chicken, grilled steak, or sautéed shrimps.
Brought to you in sizzling fajita sauce with sautéed onions, peppers,
mushrooms and tomatoes. Served with rice, beans and flour tortillas.
$ 14.95

 # 12   **DINNER AT MY FATHER'S HOUSE.**
Our 8 oz. New York shell steak grilled to your liking, topped with
red chili pepper butter. Served with cheese enchilada,
sautéed vegetables, rice and black beans.
$ 14.95

 # 13   **THE SEAWOLF SEAFOOD BURRITO**
Salmon, shrimp, scallops and calamari pan sautéed with zucchini, yellow squash,
peppers, onions and broccoli in a light sherry green tomatillo sauce.
Then folded into our large flour tortilla topped with melted cheese and salsa.
$14.95

 # 14   **MY SISTER'S WEDDING DAY DINNER**
8 oz. Grilled fish of the day served on a bed of spinach and covered
with our chilled Toucan salsa a blend of kiwi, mango,
papaya and cantaloupe. Served with black beans, rice and salad.
$ 14.95

 # 15   **THE CHIMALTENANGO TANGO**
There is a great Cantina on the way to Lago Attilan that serves this especial meal
One blue corn tostada with grilled shrimp, one grilled steak green enchilada
and one grilled red chicken relleno.
$ 14.95

 # 16   **WHY DID THE MAGICIAN'S CHICKEN**
CROSS ROUTE 212.
Chicken Breast rubbed up with our scratch spicy chipotle sauce and grilled.
Then quickly sautéed' with garlic, onion and our
almond mole' sauce in an act of kindness that answers "TO BE WITH YOU".
Served with black beans, rice, and sautéed vegetables
$ 14.95

About the Author

William Durkin was—literally—born in to the restaurant business. His mother birthed him at a family-owned restaurant in the San Francisco Bay Area, and he has worked in family-owned and other restaurants throughout his life. This crazy business helped Bill provide for himself through his college days and afterwards. The experiences and insights he gained, helped him to overcome the obstacles and failures along the way to ownership of his own successful restaurants.

Bill is currently the owner-operator of the Gypsy Wolf Cantina in Woodstock, New York.

9 780595 140831